BASIC

A Hands-on Method

SECOND EDITION

HERBERT D. PECKHAM

Professor of Natural Science
Gavilan College

McGraw-Hill Book Company

New York St. Louis San Francisco Auckland Bogotá Hamburg
Johannesburg London Madrid Mexico Montreal New Delhi Panama
Paris São Paulo Singapore Sydney Tokyo Toronto

Library of Congress Cataloging in Publication Data

Peckham, Herbert D
  BASIC: a hands-on method.

  Includes index.
  1. Basic (Computer program language) I. Title.
QA76.73.B3P4 1981   001.64'24 80-25598
ISBN 0-07-049160-7

BASIC: A Hands-on Method

Copyright © 1981, 1978 by McGraw-Hill, Inc. All rights reserved. Printed in the United States of America. No part of this publication may be reproduced, stored in a retrieval system, or transmitted, in any form or by any means, electronic, mechanical, photocopying, recording, or otherwise, without the prior written permission of the publisher.

    67890 KPKP 89876543

This book was set in Megaron by Instant Type and Graphics, Monterey, California. The editor was Charles E. Stewart; the production supervisor was Joe Campanella. The cover was designed by Joseph Gillians.
Kingsport Press, Inc., was printer and binder.

Contents

Preface to Second Edition		xi
Preface to First Edition		xiii

1 INTRODUCTION TO COMPUTERS AND BASIC — 1

- 1-1 What is BASIC? — 1
- 1-2 Where Did BASIC Originate? — 2
- 1-3 Where Is the Computer? — 2
- 1-4 Terminals — 4
- 1-5 How to Start — 6

2 INTRODUCTION TO BASIC — 9

- 2-1 Objectives — 9
  - Getting on and off the computer — 9
  - Requirements for Basic Programs — 9
  - Telling the computer What to do — 9
  - Entering and Controlling Programs — 9

- 2-2 Discovery Exercises — 10
  - Getting On and Off the Computer — 10
  - Computer Work — 12

- 2-3 Discussion — 23
  - Getting On and Off the Computer — 23
  - Requirements for BASIC Programs — 24
  - Telling the Computer What to Do — 25
  - Entering and Controlling Programs — 26

- 2-4 Practice Test — 26

v

3 COMPUTER ARITHMETIC AND PROGRAM MANAGEMENT   29

   3-1   Objectives   29
           Arithmetic on the Computer   29
           Parentheses ( ) in Computations   29
           E Notation for Numbers   29
           Variable Names in BASIC   29
           Storing and Retrieving Programs   29

   3-2   Discovery Exercises   30
           Error Correction   30
           Computer Work   32

   3-3   Discussion   46
           Arithmetic on the Computer   46
           Parentheses in Computations   49
           E Notation for Numbers   50
           Variable Names in BASIC   51
           Storing and Retrieving Programs   54

   3-4   Practice Test   56

4 INPUT, OUTPUT, AND SIMPLE APPLICATIONS   61

   4-1   Objectives   61
           Getting Numbers into a BASIC Program   61
           Printing Out Variables and Strings   61
           Spacing the Printout   61
           The REMARK Statement   61
           Simple Applications   61

   4-2   Discovery Exercises   62
           Computer Work   62

   4-3   Discussion   76
           Getting Numbers into a BASIC Program   76
           Printing out Variables and Strings   78
           Spacing the Printout   78
           The REMARK Statement   81

   4-4   Program Examples   82
           Example 1 — Unit Prices   82
           Example 2 — Converting Temperature   85
           Example 3 — Sum and Product of Numbers   86

   4-5   Problems   88

   4-6   Practice Test   94

5 DECISIONS, BRANCHING, AND APPLICATIONS — 97

- 5-1 Objectives — 97
  - Making Decisions in Programs — 97
  - Program Applications — 97
  - Finding Errors in Programs — 97

- 5-2 Discovery Exercises — 98
  - Computer Work — 98

- 5-3 Discussion — 104
  - Transfer without Conditions — 104
  - Transfer on Conditions — 105

- 5-4 Program Examples — 108
  - Example 1 — Printout of Number Patterns — 109
  - Example 2 — Automobile License Fees — 110
  - Example 3 — Averaging Numbers — 114

- 5-5 Finding Errors in Programs — 117
  - Translating BASIC Statements — 117
  - Tracing BASIC Programs — 118

- 5-6 Problems — 125

- 5-7 Practice Test — 129

6 LOOPING AND FUNCTIONS — 133

- 6-1 Objectives — 133
  - Built-in Looping — 133
  - Built-in Functions — 133
  - Program Applications — 133

- 6-2 Discovery Exercises — 134
  - Computer Work — 134

- 6-3 Discussion — 145
  - Built-in Looping — 145
  - Built-in Functions — 149

- 6-4 Program Examples — 153
  - Example 1 — Finding the Average of a Group of Numbers — 153
  - Example 2 — Temperature Conversion Table — 155
  - Example 3 — Exact Division — 156
  - Example 4 — Depreciation Schedule — 158

- 6-5 Problems — 160

- 6-6 Practice Test — 165

7 WORKING WITH COLLECTIONS OF NUMBERS — 169

- 7-1 Objectives — 169
  - Single- and Double-Subscripted Variables — 169
  - Matrix Commands — 169
  - Program Applications — 169
- 7-2 Discovery Exercises — 170
  - Subscripts — 170
  - Computer Work — 171
- 7-3 Discussion — 182
  - Single- and Double-Subscripted Variables — 182
  - Saving Space for Arrays — 184
  - Subscripted Variables and FOR NEXT Loops — 185
  - MAT Commands in BASIC — 186
- 7-4 Program Examples — 189
  - Example 1 — Examination Grades — 190
  - Example 2 — Course Grades — 193
  - Example 3 — Array Operations — 197
- 7-5 Problems — 198
- 7-6 Practice Test — 203

8 STRING VARIABLES — 207

- 8-1 Objectives — 207
  - String Input and Output — 207
  - String Functions — 207
  - String Operations — 207
- 8-2 Discovery Exercises — 207
  - Computer Work — 208
- 8-3 Discussion — 217
  - String Input and Output — 217
  - String Functions — 218
- 8-4 Program Examples — 220
  - Example 1 — String Reversal — 220
  - Example 2 — Word Count — 222
  - Example 3 — Replacement Code — 222
- 8-5 Problems — 224
- 8-6 Practice Test — 225

Contents **ix**

9 "DO-IT-YOURSELF" FUNCTIONS AND SUBROUTINES 227

9-1 Objectives 227
"Do-It-Yourself" Functions 227
Subroutines 227
Program Applications 227

9-2 Discovery Exercises 228
Computer Work 228

9-3 Discussion 236
"Do-It-Yourself" Functions 236
Subroutines 237

9-4 Program Examples 240
Example 1 — Rounding Off Dollar Values to Cents 240
Example 2 — Carpet Estimating 243

9-5 Problems 248

9-6 Practice Test 250

10 RANDOM NUMBERS AND SIMULATIONS 253

10-1 Objectives 253
Characteristics of Random-Number Generators 253
Random Numbers with Special Characteristics 253
Programming and Simulations 253

10-2 Discovery Exercises 254
Computer Work 255

10-3 Discussion 260
Random Number Generators 261
Designing Sets of Random Numbers 261
Troubleshooting Programs That Use Random Numbers 262

10-4 Program Examples 263
Example 1 — Flipping Coins 263
Example 2 — Random Integers 264
Example 3 — Distribution of Random Numbers 265
Example 4 — Birthday Pairs in a Crowd 266

10-5 Problems 267

10-6 Practice Test 269

APPENDIX A — COMPUTER SYSTEM COMMANDS 270

APPENDIX B — GLOSSARY 279

PRACTICE TEST SOLUTIONS 284

SOLUTIONS TO ODD-NUMBERED PROBLEMS 291

INDEX 305

Preface to the Second Edition

Several important changes have been made in the second edition of this book in response to suggestions received from users of the first edition. The most significant is the inclusion of a new chapter on strings and string operations. Since string operations are handled differently on various computers, a method had to be found to discuss the subject without causing confusion in the mind of the student. The strategy that was selected is to use lower-case substitution functions in BASIC statements. The student then replaces the substitution functions with the functions appropriate to the computer which is being used. These substitutions are contained in Appendix A.

The number of problems has been approximately doubled. The additional problems include some that are very easy and some that should prove quite challenging. The intent has been to increase the range of difficulty while increasing the number of problems.

The final change of note is the inclusion of a glossary in Appendix B. The purpose of this glossary is to pull together definitions, concepts, and features of BASIC in one location for easy reference by students.

Since the publication of the first edition, the small personal computer has exploded onto the marketplace. While this book was originally intended for use on time-sharing computers, it has been used very successfully on personal computers such as the Apple. Appendix A contains a blank form which, if filled out, can adapt the book to nearly any of the small computers that are now available.

HERBERT D. PECKHAM

Preface to the First Edition

This book grew out of a sense of frustration with existing BASIC programming texts intended for liberal arts students. Two characteristics of most of the texts on the market are most objectionable. First, almost all quickly begin to use mathematics at a level that excludes the vast majority of the very students we are most interested in, many of whom can rely on introductory algebra (very dimly remembered) but who need to learn how to program in BASIC. The second objection is that generally nothing in the structure of the texts requires students to spend much (if any) time on the computer. Students typically try to study programming like any other subject and do not feel the need to experiment with and execute programs on the computer. This text's main thesis is that more traditional text material should be preceded by a good deal of time experimenting with the language on the computer. The experience to date validates the idea that students work through the material more rapidly and effectively with this initial exposure to BASIC on the computer.

The intructor and student will immediately note that the structure of this book is quite different from that of most texts on the market. Each chapter begins with a statement of the objectives for that chapter. Then students are guided through a set of exercises that let them experiment with the characteristics of BASIC and see the language in action. Once students have acquired a "feel" for BASIC, they can profitably proceed to a more traditional treatment. The mathematics level has intentionally been kept very low. Students with more advanced mathematics skills can learn to use these on the computer on their own. However, if the mathematics level in the text were set too high, the majority of beginning students would become discouraged in the first few chapters. At the level presented, nearly any student should be able to work through the material without getting "hung up" by the mathematics. Students must have access to a time-sharing computer that supports the BASIC language.

The text is organized into ten chapters plus two appendices. Each chapter forms a module of instruction that should require about 2 hours of classroom time and possibly 3 or 4 hours of time outside class. Review tests are provided at the end of each chapter, enabling the student to see if the objectives have been mastered. A key explaining how to use the text material on various computers is given in Appendix A.

The text can be used in several different ways. It has been used very effectively in an open-entry, open-exit, self-paced course. If desired, the material can be presented in a traditional lecture format. Finally, it can be used with a minimum of supervision as a self-study text.

Students at any level from junior high through graduate school should be able to use the material effectively. The goal is to provide programming skills in BASIC as rapidly and effectively as possible. As indicated above, no mathematics past introductory algebra is required, and the algebra used is mainly formula evaluation. More mathematical ability is nice but unnecessary.

FOR THE INSTRUCTOR

Students must have account numbers to gain access to the computer. Certainly, the best method is to issue a different account number to each student. If desired, it is usually possible to issue a single account number to an entire class. The issue should be explored with the computer staff and settled one way or the other.

There are several advantages to having individual account numbers. When students request a listing of programs they have stored, they will see only the programs they have put there. However, if a common account number is used, all programs stored by the class will be in the same location on the computer. This may cause some confusion for the beginner. Most computers have programs that print out terminal time accumulated for each account number. If individual account numbers are used, this record provides an easy way to keep track of the time spent by individuals on the computer.

Allow about 1000 characters of storage in memory for each student. If a group account is used, all allocations should be lumped together. Some of the computer exercises require students to move programs to memory and then retrieve them. This is the purpose of the storage space in the memory.

You should check Appendix A to see if your computer is listed. If so, verify that instructions for various system commands are correct. If your computer is not included, you can easily prepare a student handout giving the proper procedures for your facility using Appendix A as a guide.

ACKNOWLEDGMENTS

The author is deeply grateful for several most valuable sources of assistance. Several dozen community college instructors in northern California have used preliminary versions of the material and provided most useful suggestions for improvement. A special vote of thanks must go to a colleague at Gavilan College, Professor John Hansell, who read the manuscript and helped eliminate the "buzz words" that crept in. Yvonne Wingo provided much needed assistance with graphics. The errors that remain are, of course, due to me.

HERBERT D. PECKHAM

1
Introduction to Computers and BASIC

Computers are now a common part of our lives. We may not see them, but they are there, involved in some way in most of our daily activities. Businesses of all sizes, educational institutions, various branches of government—none would be able to handle the bewildering quantity of information that seems to characterize our society except for computers. Only recently, however, has it become common for students at all levels to use computers routinely in their educational activities. As the price of computers continues to drop, this trend will surely continue. More and more people will need to know how to use computers if they are to participate fully in our society.

1-1 WHAT IS BASIC?

You are about to embark upon the study of a computer language called BASIC. BASIC is a very specialized language designed to permit you and the computer to understand and communicate with one another. This language is not complicated and is certainly much easier to learn than a spoken language such as Spanish or French. Even so, BASIC does have a simple vocabulary consisting of a few words, a grammatical structure, and rules of use just like any other language. Your main tasks will be to learn the vocabulary of BASIC, become used to its grammar rules, and begin to see how the language permits you to use the computer to do what you want. The level of mathematics involved has intentionally been kept very low. Therefore if you feel a bit rusty in your mathematical skills, don't be too concerned. As we proceed through BASIC, you will have an opportunity to brush up on some elementary mathematics.

A very effective way to learn about anything is to observe details and characteristics while performing a task: the "discovery" method. This is the strategy that will be used in this book. You will be asked to begin each chapter with a session on a computer terminal. After following the directions and watching closely what the computer does in response to your instructions, you will begin to acquire a "feel" for BASIC. Once you have this type of understanding, you can proceed more profitably to study written material that summarizes what you have learned. Thus, the directed exercise on a computer terminal is a key part of learning about BASIC as presented in this book.

1-2 WHERE DID BASIC ORIGINATE?

The original version of BASIC was designed and written at Dartmouth College under the direction of Professors John G. Kemeny and Thomas E. Kurtz. In September 1963 work began on a project to perfect the concept of time sharing on a computer and to create a programming language written from the user's point of view. A very interesting sidelight was that much of the actual programming on the project was done by undergraduate students at Dartmouth. The birthday of BASIC is May 1, 1964, so the language is still a teen-ager.

The success of this pioneering effort at Dartmouth soon attracted national attention, and very quickly other institutions became interested. The rest is history. Today nearly every time-sharing computer supports the BASIC language. BASIC itself has grown significantly in both power and capability from its early versions. Each year the percentage of total computer activities done in BASIC increases. What started as a project at a single college is now an established part of the computer industry throughout the world.

The most recent innovation is the emergence of small, inexpensive personal computers. Without exception, these computers can be programmed in BASIC. The BASIC that you will study in this book is reasonably transportable and can be run with minor changes on the new personal computers.

1-3 WHERE IS THE COMPUTER?

Your contact with the computer will be through a computer terminal with a typewriter-like keyboard. You can send instructions and messages to the computer by typing on the keyboard. Likewise, the computer can send information to you by typing out on your terminal. It makes very little difference where the computer itself is. It could be right beside your terminal (or, what with the astonishing decrease in size, inside your terminal!), in the next room, or halfway around the world. All that is necessary is that messages can flow back and forth between the computer and your terminal. These messages can pass over wires, through phone circuits, via radio transmission, or even by transmission of signals via satellites in orbit.

As you look around the terminal room, you will more than likely notice other people working at terminals. Each terminal is not connected to its own private computer, as this could be quite expensive. Instead, the terminals are usually connected to the same computer. The computer handles all the terminals, giving its attention briefly to each of the users while moving quickly from one terminal to the next. This happens so rapidly that you may feel you have the entire computer to yourself. Machines like this are known as time-sharing computers and can handle from a few terminals to several hundred at the same time, depending on size and cost(see Figures 1 and 2).

Quite often, introductory computer programming texts spend a considerable amount of time on the hidden workings and inner mechanisms of computers. This will not be done in this book. As a typical user, you are most likely interested in learning how to use the computer rather than the details of how it works. In precisely the same sense, you do not need to be an expert on internal combustion engines to drive an automobile! Consequently we will pursue one, and only one, goal throughout the book: how to write and execute programs in BASIC.

Even though we will not become involved with the specifics of computer construction, we should pause to note the astonishing changes that have taken place in computers in the past ten years. What was once a giant power-gobbling electronic monster can now be placed on a tiny chip. We have just begun to see the

Figure 1 Large time-sharing computer, DECsystem-10. (*Copyright © 1976 by Digital Equipment Corp. All rights reserved.*)

changes in our lives that this sophisticated technology will bring about. An entire industry exists today to build and distribute the semiconductor devices that are so common but were unknown just a few years ago. Within a few years, small computers on chips will be used in all automobiles to monitor and control various functions (see Figure 3). Probably the one thing that we can count on is that computers of all sizes and with many different characteristics will become more and more common.

4 BASIC: A Hands-on Method

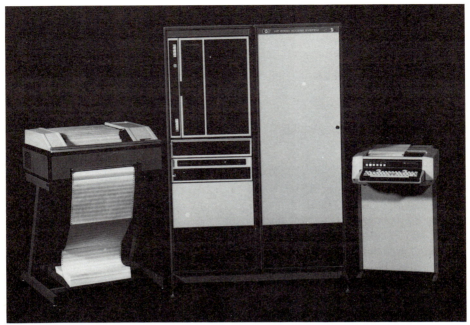

Figure 2 Small time-sharing computer, Hewlett Packard 2000 System.
(*Courtesy of Hewlett Packard Co.*)

1-4 TERMINALS

There are three different kinds of computer terminals in general use today. The first is the printing (or hard-copy) terminal, which prints the results on paper. Probably The Teletype terminal (Figure 4) was the first hard copy terminal in general use. Newer types of hard-copy terminals are more common now. The advantage of a printing terminal is that you have a record of your work with the computer which can be saved for later use (see Figure 5).

A second type of terminal is the CRT (which stands for cathode ray tube) terminal (Figure 6). Instead of a printed copy on paper, this terminal shows the output on a television-like screen (the cathode ray tube). Sometimes it is possible for you to use a separate machine to make a paper copy of whatever appears on the face of your CRT terminal.

Finally, there are graphic terminals. These look like ordinary CRT terminals but can also draw lines to produce pictures, charts, and graphs. It is this ability that leads to the name "graphic" terminal. Since we will not become involved with graphics in this book, if you find a graphic terminal use it as a CRT terminal and we will ignore the graphics ability.

The specific details of use may vary slightly from terminal to terminal. The differences are slight, however, and you should have little difficulty adapting to the different types that may be found.

Introduction to Computers and BASIC 5

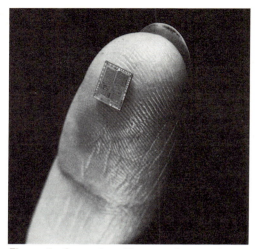

Figure 3   Computer chip on a finger. (*Photograph courtesy of Intel.*)

Figure 4   Model 33 teletype terminal. (*Photograph courtesy of Teletype Corp.*)

6 BASIC: A Hands-on Method

Figure 5 DECwriter II hard-copy terminal. (*Copyright © 1976 by Digital Equipment Corp. All rights reserved.*)

1-5 HOW TO START

You should approach each chapter in the book in the same way. The material has been organized with special learning patterns in mind, and any changes will make the process less effective and require more of your time.

Each chapter begins with a brief statement of the objectives. These should be studied carefully so you can get a clear picture of precisely what is to be done. (It's nice to know where you're going!) When asked , you should record the computer output in the space provided. Occasionally you will be asked to answer questions. The purpose of this activity is to lead you through the ideas involved and let you see BASIC working. It is important that you try to think about what will happen in situations that will be set up. This is an active relationship between you and the computer and should not be slighted. Whether or not your answers are correct is not important. The important thing is that you think carefully about the questions and try to answer. Time spent in this activity will save you time later on.

Typical programs are included in each chapter. These are discussed in great detail to point out how elements of programming are pulled together to produce a BASIC program. Each chapter past Chapter 3 has a collection of problems. You should plan to work enough problems to satisfy yourself that you can write programs at the level appropriate to each chapter. Solutions to the odd-numbered problems are at the end of the book.

Figure 6   Hewlett Packard 2644 CRT terminal. (*Photograph courtesy of Hewlett Packard Co.*)

2 Introduction to BASIC

Since your first contact with the computer may seem a bit strange and complicated, we will proceed very slowly. Rest assured that after a few sessions at the computer terminal, routine operations will seem very natural and will cause you no trouble. Initially, though, be prepared for a certain "confusion quotient."

2-1 OBJECTIVES

In this chapter we will master some simple but important concepts. These are as follows.

Getting On and Off the Computer

Since the computer manufacturers do not do this the same way, there will be more differences between computers here than anywhere else in the book. Instructions for getting on and off the computer are summarized in Appendix A.

Requirements for BASIC Programs

All BASIC programs have common characteristics. We will look at some very simple programs to learn about these.

Telling the Computer What to Do

System commands are used to tell the computer to do something to or with a BASIC program. Again, like getting on and off the computer, these system commands may be different for different computers. The system commands for various computers are also summarized in Appendix A.

Entering and Controlling Programs

Apart from system commands, we need to be able to load programs into the computer and control them while they are running. These commands also depend on the brand of computer. A summary is contained in Appendix A.

2-2 DISCOVERY EXERCISES

Before beginning work on a computer terminal, we must establish several important points. On a typewriter, a lower-case "L" is used for the numeral 1. A different key is used, however, on computer terminals. The numeral 1 is found with the other numeral keys. Consequently, one of the most frequent mistakes made at first is to use the lower-case "L" for the numeral 1. Next, do not use either the lower or upper-case letter "o" for the numeral 0. Like the numeral 1, the 0 on the computer terminal is found with the other numeral keys.

In the instructions that will follow, when you see <CR> press the RETURN key on your terminal. (On some terminals this may be the END OF LINE key.) If in the instructions a small "c" appears above and after a character, you should hold the CONTROL(or CTRL) key down while typing the character. Thus, "$A^cB^cC^c$" means to hold the CONTROL key down while typing the characters "A," "B," and "C."

Getting On and Off the Computer

The first task is to learn how to sign on and off the computer. To do this, you will need an account number. Find out what your account number is and record below for reference.

MY ACCOUNT NUMBER IS _____

Next, record the manufacturer and model of the computer you will be using.

```
COMPUTER MANUFACTURER _____ ____
MODEL _____
```

Refer to Appendix A and determine how to sign on and off your computer. Record this information below for your use.

```
SIGN-ON INSTRUCTIONS _____
_____
_____

SIGN-OFF INSTRUCTIONS _____
_____
_____
_____
```

12   BASIC: A Hands-on Method

Now that all the preliminary details are out of the way, we are ready to begin working on the computer.

Computer Work

1. Find a terminal not in use and turn it on. If you have any difficulty, get help from someone in the terminal room or from the computer center staff.

2. Sign on the computer using the instructions you looked up. If you are successful, the computer will type out a welcoming message and will indicate that it is ready for business by typing READY or some similar message. If you have difficulties getting on the computer, ask for help. Usually, if mistakes are made at this point they will persist and you will waste valuable time.

3. Type

    100 LET A=1   <CR>

    Remember that <CR> means to press the RETURN key on your terminal (this may be END OF LINE on some terminals). The line that we have typed in is the first statement of a BASIC program.

4. Type in the balance of the program as listed below.

    110 LET B=8   <CR>
    120 LET C=A+B   <CR>
    130 PRINT C   <CR>
    140 END   <CR>

    If you make mistakes while typing in the program, simply retype the line involved.

5. We now want to get a clear copy of the program the computer is storing in your work space. Look up how to display the program contained in your work space on the computer (Appendix A) and record the command below.

    TO DISPLAY THE PROGRAM IN MY WORK

    SPACE, TYPE _____

Introduction to BASIC   **13**

6. All right, now display the program in your work space on the computer. If you have done everything correctly, you should see the following program typed out on your terminal:

```
100 LET A=1
110 LET B=8
120 LET C=A+B
130 PRINT C
140 END
```

7. The statements numbered 100, 110, 120, and 130 form a very simple BASIC program. We will use this program to experiment with some of the characteristics of BASIC. For the moment, ignore the line numbers at the left of each statement. Just read the statements and try to figure out what will happen if the computer carries out the instructions in the lines. What do you think will happen?

_____

8. To find out if you are right, we must tell the computer to carry out the instructions. Using Appendix A, look up the command that will cause the computer to execute the program in your work space. Record the command below.

> TO EXECUTE THE PROGRAM IN WORK
>
> SPACE TYPE _____

Now execute the program in work space. What happened?

_____

14 BASIC: A Hands-on Method

9. Type

$$\text{100 LET A=2} \qquad \text{<CR>}$$

Display the program in work space. What has happened? (Hint: Compare this new listing of the program to the initial listing.) If you have forgoten how to display the program in work space, refer to step 5 in the computer work.

_____

10. If we execute the program now, what do you think will happen?

_____

Try it. Execute the program and record what did happen. The command to execute the program is recorded in step 8.

_____

11. Now type

$$\text{140} \qquad \text{<CR>}$$

Display the program in work space. What has changed?

_____

Introduction to BASIC **15**

12. If we execute the program now, what do you think will happen?

    _____

    See if you were right. Execute the program and record what happened.

    _____

    (Note: Some computers will execute the program even if the END statement is missing.)

13. Based upon what you have seen, the evidence is strong that there must be a certain statement at the conclusion of a BASIC program. What is this statement?

    _____

14. Let's take time out for a short review.

    a. How do you sign on your computer?

    _____

    b. What command is used to display the program in work space?

    _____

    c. How do you replace a line in a program?

    _____

16 BASIC: A Hands-on Method

d. How do you delete a line in a program?

_____

If you have any trouble with these questions, refer back to the place you copied down the various instructions or saw the process take place.

15. Now let's experiment a bit more. Sometimes we want to clear out the program in the work space on the computer. Using Appendix A, look up how to do this on your computer and record that command below.

```
┌─────────────────────────────────────────────┐
│  TO CLEAR OUT THE PROGRAM IN WORK SPACE     │
│                                             │
│  TYPE  _____    │
│                                             │
└─────────────────────────────────────────────┘
```

Using the command you have just looked up, clear out the program in your work space. Remember that you must signal the computer that you are through typing by pressing the RETURN key. What did the terminal do after you pressed the RETURN key?

_____

Execute the program in work space. What happened?

_____

What has happened to your program?

_____

Introduction to BASIC   17

If you try to display the program in work space now, what do you think will happen?

_____

Try it and record what happened.

_____

16. We have learned how to get rid of a program in work space, but now have no program left. To get our program back, we must enter it again. Type in the program below.

```
100 LET A=1        <CR>
110 LET B=8        <CR>
120 LET C=A+B      <CR>
130 PRINT C        <CR>
140 END            <CR>
```

Display the program in work space and make sure it is the same as the one above. If any corrections are needed, retype the lines involved, including the line numbers.

17. Now type

```
125 LET D=B-A      <CR>
135 PRINT D        <CR>
```

Display the program in work space. What has happened?

18. If we execute this new program, what do you think will happen?

_____

18 BASIC: A Hands-on Method

See if you were right. Execute the program and record the results below.

_____

19. In the original program, the line numbers were not consecutive (like 100, 101, 102, 103, etc.) but had gaps (e.g., 100, 110, 120, and 130). Can you think of a reason for doing this? (Hint: See step 17.)

_____

20. How do you insert lines in a BASIC program? (Hint: See steps 17 and 19.)

_____

21. Clear the program from your work space. Now type in the program below.

```
100 INPUT A         <CR>
110 LET B=A+2       <CR>
120 PRINT B         <CR>
130 GOTO 100        <CR>
140 END      <CR>
```

Display the program you have entered and make sure it is correct. If errors are noted, retype the lines.

22. This new program has several features that you have not seen before. Study the program carefully and try to think ahead to what will happen if we execute the program. Now execute the program and record what happened.

_____

Type

6   <CR>

Introduction to BASIC   19

What happened?

_____

Type

                        10   <CR>

What happened?

_____

23. What line in the program is generating the question mark?

_____

Describe in your own words what the program is doing.

_____

24. Suppose that we now decide to quit and try to sign off the computer. Refer back to the introductory section of this chapter and see how to sign off your computer. Sign off the computer by typing the command you have just looked up. Remember that you must press the RETURN key to tell the computer you are through typing. What happened?

_____

20   BASIC: A Hands-on Method

25. Probably you expected some message from the computer that it was signing off. The reason you didn't get this message was that the computer was still at line 100 in the program we entered, waiting for a number to be typed in. When you typed in the sign-off command, the computer didn't recognize this as a number and gave you the response you recorded above. The problem is that we are "hung up" in a loop. If we type in a number, the computer will go through the program, loop right back and wait for another number to be typed in. If we type anything else, the computer won't recognize it. Therefore we must have a way to get out of the loop. Using Appendix A, look up the way to jump your computer out of a loop. Record it below.

> TO JUMP THE COMPUTER OUT OF AN
>
> INPUT LOOP TYPE _____

26. Now that you know how, jump the computer out of the loop. What happened?

_____

27. One final program and we will have the material in this chapter well in hand. First, clear the program from your work space. If you have forgotten how, refer to step 15. Now type in the following program:

```
100 LET A=1        <CR>
110 PRINT A        <CR>
120 LET A=A+1      <CR>
130 GOTO 110       <CR>
140 END     <CR>
```

Display the program in work space. If you have forgotten how, refer to step 5. Be sure that you have the correct program entered. If there are any errors, retype the lines involved.

28. After studying the program, record what you think will be printed out if it is executed.

_____

Introduction to BASIC **21**

Before going on, look in Appendix A to find out how to interrupt a program that is running. Record how to do this in the space provided below.

```
TO INTERRUPT A PROGRAM THAT IS
RUNNING, PRESS _____
```

Now execute the program. If you have forgotten how, refer to step 8. Record what happened.

_____

When you get tired watching what is taking place, interrupt the program using the method you wrote down above. What happened?

_____

29. Try it once more. Execute the program and after a few numbers are typed out, interrupt the program. How do you interrupt a BASIC program that is running?

_____

30. Display the program in work space. Now type

                    120LETA=A+2   <CR>

Note that no spaces are included between the characters. Display the program in work space. Check line 120. What has happened?

_____

22 BASIC: A Hands-on Method

Now type

$$120 \text{ LET A} = \text{A} + 3 \qquad <\text{CR}>$$

Note the extra space included in the statement. Display the program in work space. Check line 120. What has happened?

___

Your computer may not add or delete spaces to produce standard spacing in BASIC statements.

31. Now let's have a final short review.

   a. How do you clear a program from work space?

   ___

   b. How do you insert lines in a BASIC program?

   ___

   c. How do you sign off the computer?

   ___

   d. How do you jump the computer out of a loop?

   ___

Introduction to BASIC   23

e. How do you interrupt a program that is running?

_____

32. This concludes the computer work for this session. Sign off the computer. What happened?

_____

Turn off the terminal and go on to the balance of of the material in the chapter.

2-3 DISCUSSION

Now that you have been through the computer work at the terminal and have seen some of the features of BASIC in action, we can summarize what has taken place.

Getting On and Off the Computer

Different manufacturers have adopted their own specific methods for getting on and off the computer. Since you will generally be using only one computer this needn't cause difficulty. Simply learn the method for your computer, and after a few terminal sessions the details will become automatic.

24 BASIC: A Hands-on Method

It might be interesting for you to examine the different methods for signing on and off computers that are summarized in Appendix A. You will see that while there is substantial agreement, there are enough differences to prevent common rules.

Requirements For BASIC Programs

Several important facts about BASIC programs have been demonstrated. To have a program to use for discussion purposes, we will return to the original program used in the computer work:

```
100 LET A=1
110 LET B=8
120 LET C=A+B
130 PRINT C
140 END
```

Each BASIC program consists of a group of lines called statements. Each statement must have a line number. In the program above, there are three types of BASIC statements: LET, PRINT, and END. The first two will be treated fully in the next chapter. For the time being the use of each of these statements in the program is clear. The END statement, however, has particular significance. The last statement in a program must be the END statement and must have the highest of the line numbers. Make it a rule to use the END statement in programs even if your computer doesn't require it.

Generally the line numbers in a BASIC program are not numbered consecutively (such as 100, 101, 102, etc.). The reason is that we may want to insert additional statements later if we discover errors or want to modify the program. If the lines were numbered consecutively, changes might involve retyping the entire program. With gaps in the line numbers, statements can be inserted by simply typing in the new statements using line numbers not already in the program.

BASIC does not care in what order the lines are entered. If, for example, we type

```
140 END
120 LET C=A+B
110 LET B=8
130 PRINT C
110 LET A=1
```

and this new program is displayed, the computer will sort out the statements and display them in numerical order. In the same way, if we were to execute the program as typed above, the computer would first sort the statements into the proper order before starting execution.

You can remove a BASIC statement from the program by typing the line number and pressing the RETURN key. Thus, BASIC statements can be added, removed, or changed as desired. This ability to change programs easily is one of the powerful characteristics of BASIC.

Telling the Computer What To Do

We must make a sharp distinction between the statements in a BASIC program and system commands. System commands tell the computer to do something with a program. We have seen several of these in the computer work and will briefly review the use of each.

When you sign on the computer, a work space is automatically set aside for your use. When a BASIC program is entered, it goes into this space. Quite often you need to see the program contained in your work space. This could be because of changes made in the program, or perhaps you simply need a copy of the program. In any case, you have already looked up the command to do this on your computer. The wise programmer will make valuable use of this command. If a program doesn't work as it should, your first step should be to display the program in work space.

Often you and the computer may be in a state of mutual confusion about the program in work space. The way to resolve the issue is to have the computer furnish a copy of the program that it is executing. Use this copy to troubleshoot the program.

The work space assigned to your terminal is a temporary storage place in memory for programs. When you sign off the computer, the contents of your work space are cleared out automatically. While working on the computer, however, it is possible to get programs mixed together. Suppose you are working with one program and decide to go on to another. If you don't clear the first program out of your work space, the second program will go in right over the first with the result that parts of both programs may be in the work space. The way to avoid doing this is to be careful to clear out (or erase) a program when you are through with it.

A BASIC program is simply a set of instructions to be acted upon by the computer. However, the computer needs to be told to start this process. When the command is received, the computer goes to the lowest numbered statement in the program, carries out the instructions, goes to the next higher numbered statement, and keeps on carrying out instructions in numerical order, unless the program directs a statement to be done out of order.

Entering and Controlling Programs

So far, when you have been instructed to type in programs or commands, <CR> has been used to prompt you to press the RETURN (or END OF LINE) key on your terminal. We should pause now to see just what this does. When a program statement or a command is typed in, a signal must be sent to the computer to indicate when all the desired characters have been entered. The RETURN key signals the computer to start processing the information just entered. Now that the point is clear, there is no need to continue with the <CR> prompt in the instructions. From now on, when you are through typing a statement or command, press the RETURN key to let the computer know you are finished.

We have seen two different cases in which there was a need to control what was happening in a program. The first was when we got hung up in an input loop. The second was when a program was running and either it wouldn't stop or we wanted to interrupt it. You have already looked up the way to handle both these situations. In either case, whether you jump the computer out of an input loop or interrupt the execution of a program, the computer halts and waits for further instructions.

2-4 PRACTICE TEST

Take the test below to discover how well you have learned the objectives of Chapter 2. The answers to the practice test are given at the end of the book.

1. How do you sign on your computer?

_____

2. How do you sign off your computer?

_____

Introduction to BASIC 27

3. How do you signal the computer that you are through typing a line or instruction?

_____

4. Suppose that your computer is waiting at an INPUT statement in a program for you to enter a number. You decide instead that you want to jump the computer out of the program. How do you do this?

_____

5. How do you interrupt a program that is running on your computer?

_____

6. What is wrong with the following program?

```
100 LET A=1
110 LET B=3
120 LET C=B-A
PRINT C
130 END
```

_____

7. What is wrong with the following program?

```
100 LET Z=4
110 LET X=5
120 LET Y=X+Z
130 PRINT Y
```

_____

8. How do you remove a line from a BASIC program?

_____

9. How do you insert a line in a BASIC program?

_____

10. How do you replace a line in a BASIC program?

_____

11. How do you display the program in your work space?

_____

12. How do you command the computer to execute the program in work space?

_____

13. How do you clear out the program in work space?

_____

Computer Arithmetic and Program Management

3-1 OBJECTIVES

Now that you have learned how to sign on and off, and how to communicate with the computer, we are ready to go on to more interesting tasks.

Arithmetic on the Computer

Ultimately, all mathematics on the computer is done using the simplest arithmetic operations. It is essential to have a clear understanding of how these arithmetic operations are done.

Parentheses ( ) in Computations

As we shall see, all mathematical expressions must be typed on a single line to enter them into the computer. Some expressions can be handled this way only by organizing parts of the expressions in parentheses. Thus, the effective use of parentheses is a necessary skill.

E Notation for Numbers

The computer must deal with both very large and very small numbers. E notation is used by the computer to describe such numbers. We need to be able to recognize and interpret E notation since the computer may type out numbers in this form.

Variable Names in Basic

Since only certain combinations of characters may be used to name (or stand for) numbers in BASIC, we must know these well to avoid time-wasting error messages from the computer.

Storing and Retrieving Programs

We have already seen some system commands. Additional system commands will be introduced in this chapter which will permit us to store and retrieve programs using the computer memory.

30 BASIC: A Hands-on Method

3-2 DISCOVERY EXERCISES

The discovery exercises in this chapter introduce the characteristics of computer arithmetic. In addition, system commands for program management will be explored.

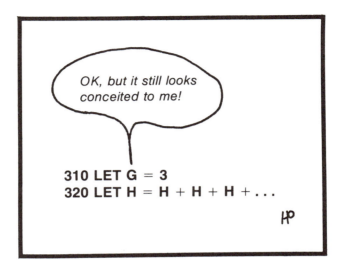

Error Correction

Since most of us make mistakes while typing, we need to be able to correct errors sent to the computer. Suppose a mistake is made while you are typing in a line. How it is corrected depends upon whether you have pressed the RETURN key yet and where the mistake is. If you press the RETURN key, the line you have been typing (mistake and all) is analyzed by the computer. Some mistakes can be picked up at this point, in which case the computer will type out various error messages.

The easiest mistake to correct is one that is noticed immediately. As an example, supposed we intended to type

```
150 PRINT B
```

but we actually type

```
150 PRIM
```

and then notice that we accidentally hit "M" rather than "N". Our problem is to correct this one character and then finish the line correctly.

Computer Arithmetic and Program Management **31**

The method used to correct errors depends on the computer. Using Appendix A, see how this is done on your computer and record the results below for reference.

```
TO DELETE A CHARACTER WHILE
TYPING _____
_____
```

In our discussion we will use <CK> to indicate the correction key. When typing, you of course will use whatever is appropriate on your computer.

Now back to the example above. If we type

<CK>NT B

The <CK> erases the "M" that was typed in error, and the rest of the statement is then entered. To further illustrate, suppose we want to type

150 PRINT C

but actually type

150 PSIN

at which point we note the "S" where the "R" should have been. We must now strike out the last three characters to correct the mistake. This is done by typing

<CK> <CK> <CK> RINT C

Using the correction key three times removes the last three characters, at which point the statement can be completed correctly.

32 BASIC: A Hands-on Method

Now suppose that the error is not noticed immediately, and we go on typing. Once noticed, it might be difficult to use the correction key the proper number of times to correct the mistake. If we haven't pressed the RETURN key yet, we can erase everything typed in the line. Look up how to do this in Appendix A and record the method below.

```
TO DELETE AN ENTIRE LINE
(BEFORE RETURN)  _____
                 _____
```

Quite often errors are not noted when lines are typed in but may show up later on when we are troubleshooting the program. In this case, the errors are corrected by simply retyping the entire line in the program.

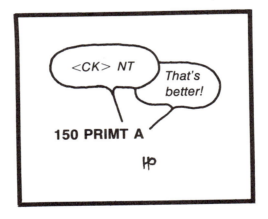

Computer Work

1. Find a free terminal and sign on your computer. Remember that you recorded the instructions to do this in Chapter 2. First we want to explore how the computer does arithmetic. Type the following program:

```
100 INPUT A
110 INPUT B
120 LET C = A+B
130 PRINT C
140 END
```

Computer Arithmetic and Program Management 33

What arithmetic operation do you think is meant by the + in line 120?

2. Check your answer by executing the program. When the computer goes to line 100, it will type out a question mark, halt, and wait for you to type in a value of A. In this case, type in 10. Don't forget that you have to press the RETURN key to let the computer know that you are through typing. The computer will then go to line 110, type out a question mark, halt, and wait for you to type in a value of B. Type in 20. What did the computer print out?

3. Now type

```
120 LET C = A-B
```

Display the program. If you execute the program and at the first question mark (INPUT prompt) type in 30 for A and the second prompt type in 12 for B, what will the computer type out?

Try it and record what was typed out.

What arithmetic operation is done with the − in line 120?

4. Type

$$120 \text{ LET } C = A*B$$

Display the program. Now execute the program and type in 5 for A and 6 for B when the INPUT prompts (question marks) come up. What did the computer type out?

_____

What arithmetic operation does the * call for?

_____

5. Type

$$120 \text{ LET } C = A/B$$

Display the program; then execute it. When the INPUT prompts come up, enter 45 for A and 15 for B. What did the computer type out?

_____

What arithmetic operation does the / call for?

_____

Computer Arithmetic and Program Management   35

6. Thus far we have seen only a single arithmetic operation on a line. Let's look at an example in which there is more than one operation. Type

$$120 \ \text{LET} \ C = A+B-B/3$$

Display the program and study it briefly. If we execute the program now and enter 2 for A and 3 for B, what do you think will be typed out?

_____

Execute the program and write down what happened.

_____

7. Clear out the program in your work space. Now type

$$100 \ \text{LET} \ A = 3*3$$
$$110 \ \text{LET} \ B = 3\uparrow2$$

You may not find the ↑ symbol in line 110 on your terminal. If not, use the ^ character which will be there. They both mean the same thing. Now finish typing in the rest of the program.

$$120 \ \text{PRINT} \ A$$
$$130 \ \text{PRINT} \ B$$
$$140 \ \text{END}$$

Display the program and make sure it is correct. Now execute the program and record what was typed out.

_____

36 BASIC: A Hands-on Method

Compare the numbers printed out to the expressions in the lines where they were computed. See if you can figure out what is taking place.

8. Type

           100 LET A = 3*3*3
           110 LET B =3^3

Execute the program. What was typed out?

_____

9. Type

           100 LET A = 2*2*2*2
           110 LET B = 2^4

Execute the program. What was typed out?

_____

What is the ↑ (or ^) symbol used for?

_____

10. Remember from your introductory algebra course (if you haven't had algebra, don't panic!) that when a number is to be multiplied by itself three times, for

Computer Arithmetic and Program Management 37

example, we can indicate this with an exponent. If the number were 2, we would write the expression as

$$2^3$$

How would this expression be written in BASIC using the ↑ (or ^) symbol? (Hint: see steps 7, 8, and 9.)

_____

11. Fill in the operators (symbols) that call for the following arithmetic operations:

Division

_____

Addition

_____

Exponentiation

_____

Subtraction

_____

Multiplication

_____

38 BASIC: A Hands-on Method

12. Clear out the program in your work space. Type

```
100 LET A = 4+2*6/3
110 LET B = (4+2)*6/3
120 LET C = 4+(2*6)/3
130 LET D = 4+2*(6/3)
140 PRINT A
150 PRINT B
160 PRINT C
170 PRINT D
180 END
```

The two points of this program are (1) the order in which the arithmetic is done, and (2) the effect of the parentheses. If you look closely it is clear that the same numbers are involved in each of the calculations in lines 100, 110, 120, and 130. The only difference is the groupings in the lines. Execute the program and record what was typed out.

Study the program and the numbers the computer typed out until you see what is taking place in the program. There are very specific rules the computer uses in such situations. We will go over these rules later in the chapter.

13. Clear out the program in your work space. Now enter the following program:

```
100 LET A = 3*100
110 LET B = 3*100*100
120 LET C = 3*100*100*100
130 PRINT A
140 PRINT B
150 PRINT C
160 END
```

Execute the program and record the output.

Computer Arithmetic and Program Management **39**

Can you explain the different form in which the numbers were typed out? (Hint: Count the number of zeros in the multipliers in lines 100, 110, and 120 in the program.)

14. Type

```
100 LET A = 4/100
110 LET B = 4/(100*100)
120 LET C = 4/(100*100*100*100)
```

Execute the program and record the output.

_____

Again, can you see what is taking place in the output? Count the zeros in the denominators in lines 100, 110, and 120.

15. If an E shows up in a number typed out by the computer, what does it mean? Explain in your own words.

_____

If you still do not fully understand the purpose of the E notation, don't worry. We will return to it later.

16. Now we must look more closely at the symbols (names) for numbers in BASIC programs. Clear out the program in your work space. Type

```
100 LET A = 1
```

So far, so good. We have seen this type of expression many times already. The letter "A" is a name for the number 1. Now type

40 BASIC: A Hands-on Method

$$\texttt{110 LET BC = 2}$$

What happened?

_____

On most newer computers, BC can be used to name a variable. On older computers, this is not so. If you received an error message use Appendix A to find out how to handle the situation on your computer. Record below.

```
FOLLOWING AN ERROR INDICATION BY THE
COMPUTER, MORE INFORMATION CAN BE
OBTAINED BY _____
_____

TO GET OUT OF THE ERROR MODE
_____
_____
```

We want to type another line, so follow the instructions above to get out of the error mode and back to BASIC.

17. Now type

$$\texttt{100 LET B1 = 2}$$

What happened?

_____

18. Type

    110 LET C28 = 3

What happened?

_____

If you get an error message, get back to BASIC using the method you wrote down above.

19. Based on what you have seen in the previous steps, it seems clear that certain names for numbers in LET statements are all right and some are not. The names "BC" and "C28" may or may not be acceptable depending on the computer "B1" will work on any computer. See if you can sum this up by filling out the imformation below.

Name	Acceptable to BASIC?
A	
B	
DOG	
B5	
T581	

20. Can a single letter be a name for a number in BASIC?

_____

Can a single letter followed by a single numeral (digit) be a name for a number in BASIC?

_____

42 BASIC: A Hands-on Method

Can anything else be used to name a number in BASIC?

_____

21. Before we can proceed, you must look up the instructions to carry out the system commands below. This information is in Appendix A. Record how to accomplish the system commands on your computer.

TO MOVE A PROGRAM FROM DISK STORAGE

TO WORK SPACE TYPE _____

_____

TO MOVE A PROGRAM FROM WORK SPACE

TO DISK STORAGE _____

_____

TO CLEAR OUT A PROGRAM IN

DISK STORAGE TYPE _____

_____

*TO NAME A PROGRAM IN WORK SPACE

TYPE

_____

TO DISPLAY A CATALOG OF PROGRAMS

STORED UNDER MY ACCOUNT NUMBER

TYPE _____

---

22. Clear out the program in your work space. Type in the following program:

Computer Arithmetic and Program Management 43

```
100 LET A = 2
110 LET B = 3
120 LET C = A*B
130 PRINT C
140 END
```

Display the program and make sure it is correct. Think of a name for this program. The name should have five or fewer characters. For the time being, let's limit the characters in the name to the letters of the alphabet. Record the name you have selected below.

_____

23. Refer to the system commands you wrote down in step 21. Name the program in work space using the name you wrote down above. If you cannot name a program in work space on your computer, ignore this step.

24. Again, refer to the system commands you recorded in step 21. Move the program in your work space to disk storage. If you couldn't name the program in step 23, it should be named now as it is moved from work space to disk storage. Display the catalog of programs stored under your account number on the disk. Is the program you just moved there on the disk?

_____

If other people are using the same account number, you may find many programs stored on the disk in addition to your program you just named. Even if you are the only user on your account number there may be additional information stored there by the computer as part of its housekeeping functions.

25. Clear out your work space. Now display a catalog of programs in disk storage under your account number. Are the programs in disk storage affected when your work space is cleared out?

_____

26. Type in the following program.

```
100 LET D = 2*6-8/4
110 PRINT D
120 END
```

Think of a name for this program. Don't use the same name you recorded in step 22. Again, limit the name to five or fewer letters of the alphabet. Record the name below.

_____

Name the program in your work space using the name you just wrote down. Move the program in work space to disk storage. Now display the program in work space. What is its name?

27. Display the catalog of programs stored in disk storage under your account number. Are the two programs you just entered there?

_____

Now, we should have two programs stored that were just entered. The name of the first program is listed in step 22; the name of the second was written in step 26. To simplify the discussion, these two programs will be referred to as "program 22" and "program 26." You, of course, must use the names you selected for the two programs.

28. Refer to the system command in step 21. Move program 22 from disk to work space. Display this program and verify that it is the right one. Now move program 26 from disk to work space. Display the program in work space. Which one is there now?

_____

Computer Arithmetic and Program Management **45**

What happened to program 22 that was in work space when we moved program 26 into work space from disk storage?

_____

29. Refer back to step 21 and look up how to clear out a program in disk storage. Clear out the program named in step 26 from memory and then display the program in work space. Which one is there?

_____

When we cleared out program 26 in disk storage, did it affect anything in work space?

_____

30. Display a catalog of the programs stored under your account number on disk. Program 26 should not be there, but program 22 should be. Inspect the listing of programs. Is everything the way it should be?

_____

31. Note that if we now clear out the work space, we will lose both the copy of program 26 in disk storage (we removed that in step 29) and the copy in work space. Clear out your work space. Display the program in work space. Is anything there?

_____

Try to move program 26 from disk to work space. What happened?

_____

46 BASIC: A Hands-on Method

Clear out program 22 from disk storage. Sign off the computer.

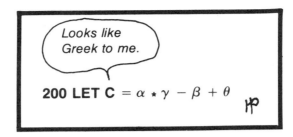

3-3 DISCUSSION

A number of very important points have been introduced in the computer work. Probably you didn't meet with too much difficulty going through the directed exercises, but this shouldn't make you ignore the fundamental ideas involved. Lack of understanding at this point will return to haunt you later on in the book. Consequently we will go over each of the objectives of the chapter in great detail to ensure that they are mastered.

Arithmetic on the Computer

We are concerned with five arithmetic operations. These are addition, subtraction, multiplication, division, and exponentiation. The first four are certainly familiar to you, and the last (exponentiation) is frightening mainly because of the fierce-looking word used to define the process. Let's go over each of these operations and see how the computer does them.

Addition and subtraction are handled on the computer precisely as you would expect. The symbols used to define the operations (+ and -) mean the same thing to the computer that they mean in mathematics classes.

Multiplication is handled the same way on the computer as in arithmetic, but has a different symbol to define the process, the * character. Thus 2*3 is 6. A*B signals the computer to look up the numbers in A and B, then multiply them together.

Division is indicated with the / symbol. A/B means to divide the number stored in location A by the one stored in B. Likewise, 8/2 means to divide 8 by 2.

Finally, the exponentiation operation is defined by the ↑ (or ^) symbol. Exponentiation merely means "raised to the power." Therefore, 3↑4 (or 3↑4) means "3 raised to the fourth power," which in turn means 3 multiplied by itself four times, giving 81 as the result.

Computer Arithmetic and Program Management

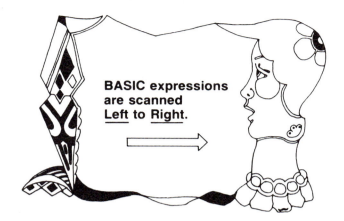

We must be very careful to understand the order in which arithmetic operations are done by the computer. An example will illustrate the point. Consider the following expression:

$$2+3\wedge2/5-1$$

If the computer simply goes through the expression from the left, performing operations as they are met, the result would be 2 plus 3 (giving 5), raised to the second power, (giving 25), divided by 5 (giving 5), minus 1 producing an answer of 4. However, suppose addition and subtraction are done first, then exponentiation, then multiplication and division. This would give 5 raised to the second power (giving 25), divided by four, for an answer of 6.25.

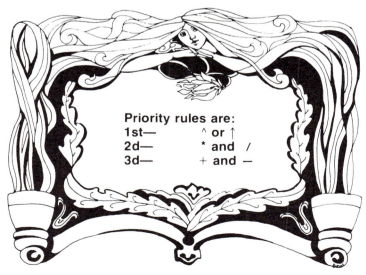

Priority rules are:
1st—   ^ or ↑
2d—   * and /
3d—   + and −

48 BASIC: A Hands-on Method

Clearly, we could go on with different rules for the order of arithmetic operations and might get different answers each time. The point is that there are well-defined rules in BASIC for the order and priority of arithmetic operations, and we must understand them. Here they are:

The order of operations is from left to right using the priority rules below.
1st: Exponentiation
2nd: Multiplication and division
3rd: Addition and subtraction

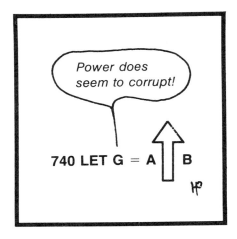

Now if we go back to our example of

$$2+3\wedge2/5-1$$

we scan left to right for any exponentiation. Since there is an exponentiation indicated (3↑2), it is done first. Now the expression is

$$2+9/5-1$$

Scanning from left to right, we look for exponentiation, and finding none, look for the operations with the next highest priority (multiplication and division). The division is therefore done next, with the following result:

$$2+1.8-1$$

Since there are no more multiplications or divisions left in the expression, we scan from left to right for addition and subtraction. The addition gives

$$3.8-1$$

and the final subtraction produces the answer of 2.8.

Review the rules for order and priority of arithmetic operations until they become second nature to you. We will look at the rules again when the use of parentheses is discussed in the next section.

Parentheses in Computations

The rules for order and priority of arithmetic operations are not the whole issue, however. There is often a bit more involved. To see this, consider the following more complicated example:

$$((2*3+4\uparrow 2)*2+5)*(3\uparrow 2-4)$$

with groups labeled A = $(2*3+4\uparrow 2)$, B = $((2*3+4\uparrow 2)*2+5)$, C = $(3\uparrow 2-4)$.

Obviously, the difference between this expression and the ones we have been studying is the use of parentheses to group parts of the expression. We will go through this example in great detail to show you how the computer attacks the arithmetic.

The computer starts by scanning from left to right and meets the left parenthesis of B. It then looks inside to see if there are any left parentheses and finds one for A. The next parenthesis met is a right parenthesis for A. At this point, the computer has isolated the first group of operations to be done. This is

$$2*3+4\uparrow 2$$

and is evaluated using the order and priority rules. The result is 22 (check it). Now our problem has become

$$(22*2+5)*(3\uparrow 2-4)$$

with groups B = $(22*2+5)$ and C = $(3\uparrow 2-4)$.

On the next scan, the computer isolates parentheses B, does the arithmetic inside, and the problem is now

$$49*(3\uparrow 2-4)$$
with C bracketing the inner expression.

Since there are only the C parentheses left, the computer does the arithmetic inside, giving

$$49*5$$

which after the final multiplication results in the answer of 245.

Thus, if parentheses are nested the computer works back out from the deepest set, working from left to right. When a set of parentheses is removed, the arithmetic operations inside are done according to the order and priority rules already given. A very good rule of thumb for the beginner to follow is that if there can possibly be any confusion about how the computer will evaluate an expression, use extra parentheses. Too many cannot harm, but too few certainly can.

E Notation for Numbers

Numbers are printed out by BASIC in different forms. In particular, numbers are sometimes printed out in what is known as the E notation. Examples of the E notation are 2.145E+06 or 6.032E-07. Now we will go back over the ideas introduced in the computer work to clarify the idea of E notation.

It is easy to see why such a special notation is needed for either very large or very small numbers. Most computers print out only six to ten digits in a number. A problem comes up if we want the computer to print out a number like 45612800000 which would require eleven digits. The computer will print this out as 4.56128E+10, which means that the decimal point belongs ten places to the right of its present position. The number 8956000000000 would be printed out as 8.956E+12. The E+12 means that the decimal point belongs twelve places to the right. We can also express very small numbers in the same way. The number 0.0000000683 would be typed out as 6.83E-08. The E-08 means that the decimal point belongs eight places to the left. The table below should help you understand how to convert from decimal to E notation or from E back to deciamal notation.

Decimal Form	E Notation
2630000	2.63E+06
263000	2.63E+05
26300	2.63E+04
2630	2.63E+03
263	2.63E+02
26.3	2.63E+01
2.63	2.63
0.263	2.63E−01
0.0263	2.63E−02
0.00263	2.63E−03
0.000263	2.63E−04
0.0000263	2.63E−05
0.00000263	2.63E−06

To change from E to decimal notation, look at the sign following the E. If the number is +, Move the decimal point to the right as many places as the number. If the sign after the E is −, move the decimal point to the left. To convert from decimal to E notation, just reverse the process.

Actually, you shouldn't get very tense about the E notation, since you will rarely use it when setting up programs on the computer. The main reason for bringing up the issue is that the computer may type out numbers in the E notation. Consequently, you should be able to recognize what is happening.

Variable Names in BASIC

Now we come to one of the ideas in BASIC that most often causes problems for the beginner. It concerns variable names and the distinction between the name of the variable and the number stored under that name. In the BASIC statement

$$100 \ \text{LET} \ A = 2$$

the A names a variable. By a variable, we mean that different values can be assigned to A. Consequently, LET statements are often called assignment statements. In this case the variable A is assigned the value 2. Actually, what is taking place is that somewhere in the computer there is a memory location named A, and the number 2 is stored in that location. The fundamental idea is to separate the name of a location in memory from the contents of the memory locations. Its the same notion as the difference between a post office box number and the contents of that box. The box number does not change, but the contents of the box may be changed at any time.

Suppose we have a BASIC statement such as

$$120 \text{ LET } B = B+1$$

You might experiment a bit to see if your computer requires the LET in the statement. If not, the computer will accept

$$120 \ B = B+1$$

However, since some computers require the LET we will always include it in the programs in this book.

Next, if we consider the statement above as an algebraic equation, we have

$$B = B+1$$

If we subtract B from both sides of this equation, we have

$$0 = 1$$

which is very strange indeed! It is certainly clear that in a BASIC statement, the = sign does not mean the same as it does in an algebraic equation. Instead, the statement

$$120 \text{ LET } B = B+1$$

instructs the computer to get the number stored in location B, add 1 to the number, and put the result back in the storage location named B. Likewise, the statement

$$130 \text{ LET } C = A+B$$

instructs the computer to get the numbers stored in locations named A and B, add them together, and put the result in the storage location named C. The equal sign means to evaluate what is on the right and assign it to the variable named on the left.

Computer Arithmetic and Program Management

If we store a number in a location, anything that was stored there before is lost. Consider the following statements:

```
100 LET A = 1
110 LET A = 2*3
```

Line 100 instructs the computer to set up a location called A and put the number 1 in that location. Line 110 tells the computer to multiply 2 by 3 and store the product in location A. Note carefully that the 1 stored previously in location A has been lost.

This brings us to the heart of the issue. The letter A, which identifies a location, is called a variable because the contents of A can be changed. The name of the location does not change, but the number stored there can be.

In BASIC, the names that can be used for variables depends upon the computer. Some will permit names like TAXES or PROFIT. Names like these are useful in that they identify the quantity named. You may wish to experiment with your computer to see if names like these are permitted.

All computers permit the use of a single letter or a single letter followed by a single digit. We will follow this naming convention in this book to avoid confusion.

There is another type of variable called a string variable. The variable names a string of characters rather than a number. This variable type will be discussed fully in Chapter 8.

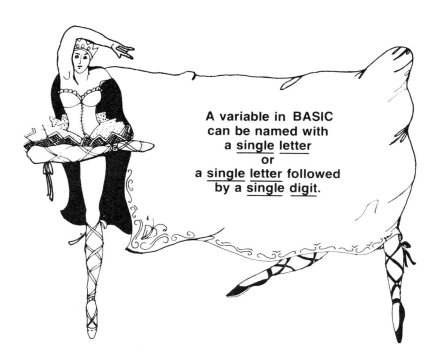

A variable in BASIC can be named with a <u>single letter</u> or a <u>single</u> letter followed by a <u>single</u> <u>digit</u>.

54 BASIC: A Hands-on Method

Let's go over the important points once more. A variable name in BASIC identifies a storage location in memory that can contain a number. The contents of the storage location (the value of the variable) may be changed, but the name of the location cannot. The names that we will use in BASIC are either a single letter or a single letter followed by a single digit. The LET (or assignment) statement evaluates what is on the right side of the equal sign and assigns it to the storage location named on the left side. Thus,

```
100 LET D = A+B+C
```

instructs the computer to evaluate the expression (A+B+C) using the numbers stored in locations A, B, and C. The results are then stored in the location named D.

Storing and Retrieving Programs

If every time we signed on a computer, we had to type in programs that we wanted to use, very little work would get done on computers. One of the nice characteristics of time-sharing computers is that we can type in long or complicated programs, troubleshoot them, and then store the programs on the computer for future reference. We need only sign on the computer and can then retrieve any of the programs that have been previously stored.

To understand what the program-management system commands do, it is necessary to see how individual users are handled by the computer. As you learned before, when you sign on the computer, you are allocated a block of memory called a work space. This is where the programs go which you type in from the terminal. Of course, there may be many users on the computer at any given time. Each of the users is assigned a work space. The computer works briefly on the task contained in a work space, then goes on to the next work space, and so on. This all happens so rapidly that you may believe there are no other users on the computer.

The problem is that when we sign off the computer, all the material in our work space is lost. We need to be able to move programs from work space to permanent memory storage where they can be retrieved if needed. You have already copied the procedure for various program-management system commands for your computer. Refer to step 21 in the computer work to review this.

You can't move a copy of a program from your work space to disk storage unless it has been named. Once named, it can be moved to a disk and stored under your account number. At any later time, after you sign on, you can ask the computer to move this program from disk storage into work space where it will once more be available to you.

Of course, we might not want to keep a specific program on a disk forever. A system command is provided to clear our programs from disk storage. If you move a copy of a program from memory into work space and then clear out the copy in disk storage, the copy in work space is not touched. Likewise, you can have one program

Computer Arithmetic and Program Management 55

in workspace and clear out another program in disk storage without changing the first.

We should discuss an interesting problem that occurs in program management. Suppose you have a program named DOG in disk storage. You sign on the computer and move a copy of DOG from disk storage to your work space. Note that the name DOG comes into work space with program. Then we make changes in the program. The computer records the fact that the program in work space has been changed. If we now try to move DOG back to the disk, we will get an error message from the computer saying that there is a duplicate program entry. If we think about it a bit, we could have expected this. We have a program called DOG on the disk and a different program called DOG in work space. Since the computer cannot store two different programs with the same name under a single account number, it will refuse to move the changed copy of DOG from work space to disk storage.

The problem is easy to solve. We simply delete the program called DOG from disk storage. Remember that this was the old copy of the program. Next, we move the modified copy of DOG from work space to disk. But now, since there is no program named DOG on the disk, the transfer is completed. This, then, is how to change a program stored in disk storage. Transfer the program from the disk to work space and make the necessary changes. Clear out the copy of the program on the disk. Then move the modified copy of the program from work space to disk storage.

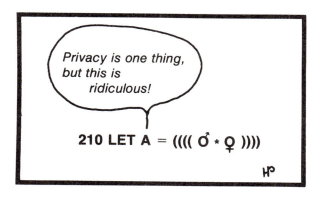

Probably in this introductory course you won't have enough programs in disk storage to cause much worry about the abililty to get a catalog of programs stored under your account number. The serious programmer, however, may need to have many programs stored on the computer and used from time to time. In such situations it is difficult to remember precisely what you have stored. Hence, it is very useful to be able to instruct the computer to give you a catalog of the programs stored under your account number. If you are the only person using your account number, the only programs stored on disk will be the ones you have put there. However, if a number of other users are on the same account number, a catalog of programs stored will likely contain many programs in addition to yours.

3-4 PRACTICE TEST

The practice test that follows is provided for you to check how well you have learned the key points and objectives of the chapter. Check your answers against the key given at the end of the book.

1. Write down the symbols that are used to carry out the following arithmetic operations in BASIC expressions:

   a. Subtraction

   _____

   b. Multiplication

   _____

   c. Addition

   _____

   d. Exponentiation

   _____

   e. Division

   _____

2. When evaluating arithmetic expressions, there is a priority of operations. What is this priority?

a. 1st

_____

b. 2nd

_____

c. 3rd

_____

3. When scanning arithmetic expressions, the computer searches in a specific direction. What is this direction

_____

4. Write a BASIC statement to evaluate the following expression. Number the line 100.

$$A = (4 + 3B/D)^2$$

_____

5. If the following program is executed, what will be typed out?

```
100 LET A = 2
110 LET B = 3
120 LET C = (A*B+2)/2
```

58 BASIC: A Hands-on Method

```
130 PRINT C
140 END
```

6. Convert the following numbers to E notation:

   a. 5160000

   b. 0.0000314

7. Convert the following numbers to decimal notation.

   a. 7.258E+06

   b. 1.437E-03

8. In the expression below, give the order in which the operations will be done by the computer.

```
100 LET A = (6/3+4)^2
```

9. What are the names for variables that are permissible in BASIC?

_____

10. Write down how to carry out the following system commands on your computer:

   a. Move a program from disk storage to work space

   _____

   b. Move a program from work space to disk storage

   _____

   c. Clear out a program in disk storage

   _____

   d. Clear out a program in work space

   _____

   e. Display the program in work space

   _____

   f. Execute the program in work space

   _____

60 BASIC: A Hands-on Method

   g. Display a catalog of programs under your account number

___

11. Suppose you are typing a line into the computer and have not yet pressed RETURN. How do you

   a. Correct a single character

___

   b. Delete everything typed in

___

Input, Output, and Simple Applications

4-1 OBJECTIVES

In this chapter we will get down to the business of writing programs. We will also increase our knowledge of BASIC by looking at some details about input and output. The objectives are as follows.

Getting Numbers into a BASIC program

There are only three ways that we can enter numbers into the computer for a BASIC program. Since the computer is concerned mainly with numbers, we need to understand how to input these numbers.

Printing Out Variables and Strings

After information is computed, it must be printed out. Different choices are available for the kind of output. Usually we will want to output strings of characters as well as numbers. This string output is handled essentially the same as numbers, but needs special attention.

Spacing the Printout

The previous objective is concerned with the output of numbers and strings of characters. Here we are concerned with the spacing of that output.

The REMARK Statement

The wise programmer includes comments in programs to help explain or interpret what is being done. The REMARK statement in BASIC permits us to do this.

Simple Applications

Our ultimate goal is to learn how to write and troubleshoot programs. In this chapter we will begin with some modest program assignments.

62 BASIC: A Hands-on Method

4-2 DISCOVERY EXERCISES

The necessary preliminary details have already been seen to. Therefore, we can proceed directly to the computer work to explore the objectives of the chapter.

Computer Work

1. Sign on the computer. Enter the following program:

```
100 INPUT A
110 INPUT B
120 INPUT C
130 LET D = A+B+C
140 PRINT D
150 END
```

What do you think will happen if we execute this program?

___

Execute the program. When the first question mark is typed out (the INPUT prompt for A), type in 2 Likewise, when the second question mark comes up, type in 3, and finally, at the last question mark, type in 5. Record what happened below.

___

2. Note that in the program in step 1 we have three INPUT statements (lines 100, 110, and 120). Type

```
100
110
```

What does this do to the program?

___

Input, Output, and Simple Applications **63**

Display the program in work space and see if you are right. Then type

```
120 INPUT A,B,C
```

Display the program. What has happened?

_____

3. Execute the program and when the INPUT prompt (?) is output, type in

```
2,3,5
```

What happened?

_____

Can you input more than one variable at a time in a BASIC program?

_____

4. Execute the program, and when the INPUT prompt is output, type

```
2,3
```

What happened?

_____

64 BASIC: A Hands-on Method

What is the computer waiting for?

_____

Type

5

and record below what happened.

_____

5. Execute the program and when the INPUT prompt appears, type

2,3,5,1

What happened?

_____

6. Can you type in more numbers than called for at an INPUT statement?

_____

What will happen if you do?

_____

Input, Output, and Simple Applications **65**

7. Can you type in fewer numbers than called for at an INPUT statement?

What will happen if you do?

---

8. Type

   120 READ A,B,C

Display the program. What has happened?

Execute the program and record what happened.

---

9. Now type

   125 DATA 2,3,5

and display the program. What has happened?

---

66 BASIC: A Hands-on Method

10. Execute the program and record what happened.

_____

Based upon what you have just seen, anytime a BASIC program contains a READ statement, there must be another type of statement in the program. What is that statement?

_____

11. Name two different methods (other than using a LET statement) for getting numbers into a program. (Hint: See steps 2 and 8.)

_____

12. Display the program in work space. Delete the DATA statement. Type

        145 DATA 2,3,5

and display the program again. What has happened?

_____

13. Execute the program and record the output.

_____

Does it appear to make any difference where the DATA statement is in the program?

14. Clear out the program in your work space. Enter the program below

```
100 READ A,B
110 LET C = A/B
120 PRINT C
130 GOTO 100
140 DATA 2,1,6,2,90,9,35,7
150 END
```

What do you think will happen if you execute the program?

___

Try it and see if you were correct. Record the output.

___

Is the "out of data" message associated with the READ statement or the DATA statement?

___

15. Delete the DATA statement in line 140 from the program. Now enter the following statements:

```
105 DATA 10,2
115 DATA 100,50
125 DATA 50,5
```

Display the program in work space. What has taken place?

___

68 BASIC: A Hands-on Method

16. If we execute the program, what do you think will be typed out?

_____

Execute the program and see if you were correct. Record the output below.

_____

17. Can you have more than one DATA statement in a BASIC program?

_____

Does it seem to make any difference where the DATA statements are in the program?

_____

18. Clear out the program in work space. Enter the following program:

```
100 LET A = 10
110 PRINT A
120 END
```

What will happen if you execute this program?

_____

Input, Output, and Simple Applications 69

Execute the program and record what took place.

_____

19. Now type

    110 PRINT "A"

and display the program in work space. What has happened?

_____

What will happen if we execute the program?

_____

Execute the program and record what the computer typed out.

_____

20. Type

    110 PRINT "HOUND DOG = ";A

and display the program in work space. What do you think will happen if we execute this program?

_____

70 BASIC: A Hands-on Method

Execute the program and record what did happen.

_____

21. Now let's try a different wrinkle. Type

> 110 PRINT "B = ";A

Display the program and study it carefully. If we execute the program, what do you think will happen?

_____

Try it and see if you were right. Record the output below.

_____

22. Type

> 95 REM DEMO PROGRAM

Display the program. What has happened?

_____

Execute the program. What was the output?

_____

Input, Output, and Simple Applications 71

Does the REM statement in line 95 have any effect on the program?

_____

23. Clear out the program in your work space. Enter the following program:

```
100 REM METRIC CONVERSION PROGRAM
110 REM CONVERT LBS TO GRAMS
120 PRINT "INPUT NO. OF LBS.";
130 INPUT P
140 LET G = 454*P
150 PRINT P;" POUNDS IS ";G;"GRAMS"
160 GOTO 120
170 END
```

Display the program and verify it is correct. Study the program carefully and try to guess what will happen if it is executed. Now execute the program. When the INPUT prompt is typed out, enter any number you desire. Note what is typed out. Repeat this process several times, then jump the computer out of the INPUT loop. If you have forgotten how, see Chapter 2, step 25, of the computer work. What is the purpose of the REM statement?

_____

24. Type

```
115 INPUT P
130
160 GOTO 115
```

and then display the program in work space. What has happened?

_____

72 BASIC: A Hands-on Method

Will the program work in this form?

_____

Execute the program and at the INPUT prompt, type 1. What happened?

_____

Jump the program out of the INPUT loop.

25. Let's experiment with this program a bit more. Clear out the program in work space and enter it again, modified as follows:

```
100 REM METRIC CONVERSION PROGRAM
110 REM CONVERT LBS. TO GRAMS
120 PRINT "INPUT NO. OF LBS.";
130 INPUT P
140 PRINT P;"POUNDS IS ";G;"GRAMS"
150 LET G = 454*P
160 GOTO 120
170 END
```

Can the program be executed in this form?

_____

Execute the program and at the INPUT prompt, type 2. What happened?

_____

Explain in your own words what is wrong. Remember that if a variable is not defined initially in your program, your computer may set it equal to 0.

_____

Input, Output, and Simple Applications 73

26. Clear out the program in work space. Enter the following program:

```
100 READ A
110 PRINT A
120 GOTO 100
130 DATA 10,12,8,9,73,60,82
140 END
```

Execute the program and record what happened.

_____

27. Type

```
110 PRINT A,
```

Note that all we have done is to insert a comma after the A in line 110. Execute the program and record what happened.

_____

28. Now replace the comma after A with a semicolon by typing

```
110 PRINT A;
```

Execute the program and record what happened.

_____

74 BASIC: A Hands-on Method

29. If a variable in a PRINT statement is not followed by any punctuation marks, what happens after the number is printed out? (Hint: See step 26.)

_____

Suppose the variable is followed by a comma?

_____

What will happen if the variable is followed by a semicolon?

_____

30. Clear out the program in your work space and enter the following program:

```
100 LET A = 20
110 READ B
120 PRINT TAB(A);B;
130 LET A = A+10
140 GOTO 110
150 DATA 1,2,3
160 END
```

Execute the program and record what happened.

_____

31. Type

```
130 LET A = A+5
```

Input, Output, and Simple Applications **75**

Execute the program and record what happened.

_____

32. Type

$$130 \text{ LET } A = A+20$$

Execute the program and record what happened.

_____

33. What does the TAB in the print statement appear to control?

_____

34. This concludes the computer work for now. Sign off the computer.

4-3 DISCUSSION

In this chapter we have begun to get away from the mere mechanics of controlling the computer. Instead we will concentrate more on writing and troubleshooting programs. This skill doesn't come naturally to most students, and consequently we will give the topic a great deal of attention, both now and in later chapters.

Getting Numbers into a BASIC Program

In Chapter 2 we saw one way to get numbers into a program. That was by assigning values to a variable in the program itself. For example,

```
100 LET A = 6
```

introduces the value 6 into a program and stores the number under the variable name A. This method has limitations. We need to examine other ways in which numbers can be introduced into a BASIC program.

Let's look first at the INPUT statement and how it is used. An example might be

```
260 INPUT G
```

When the computer executes this line, it will type out a question mark as a prompt that input is expected from the terminal, then will halt and wait for you to type in the number. In the case above, the number typed in will be known as G.

More than one variable may be called for in a single INPUT statement, such as

```
420 INPUT A,B,C,D
```

In this case the same INPUT prompt (the question mark) is typed out, but now the computer is expecting four numbers to be typed in, separated by commas. If only three numbers are entered and the RETURN key pressed, the computer will come back with a prompt for more input since it is still looking for an additional number. If more than four numbers are typed in initially, the computer will use the first four as called for in the program, but may warn you that additional input of data was detected.

The last method of providing for numerical input into the computer is with the READ and DATA statements. The statement

```
100 READ A,B,C,D
```

is handled by the computer the same as the INPUT statement with two exceptions. First, the computer does not stop. There is no need to, as will be seen. The second exception is that the numbers called for are read from DATA statements contained within the program rather than being entered at the terminal in response to an INPUT prompt.

To illustrate the READ and DATA statements, consider the following program:

```
100 READ A,B,C,D
110 LET E = A+B+C+D
120 PRINT E
130 DATA 25,3,17,12
140 END
```

The program reads four numbers from the DATA statement and prints out the sum of the numbers. It makes no difference where the DATA statement is in the program except that the END statement still must be the highest numbered statement. There can be more than one DATA statement, and they need not be grouped together at the same place in the program. As numbers are called for by READ statments, they are taken in order from the DATA statements, beginning with the lowest numbered statement. Should numbers be requested after all have been used from the available DATA statements, the computer will type an "out of data" message and then halt.

To sum up, there are three methods by which numbers can be introduced into BASIC programs. They are using (1) LET statements, (2) the INPUT statement, and (3) the READ and DATA statements. There are times when each of these methods can be used to advantage. You will become familiar with the advantages and disadvantages of each method as we spend more time writing programs.

Output from the computer is quite simple. The computer can print out either the numerical value of a variable (a number) or a string of characters. To illustrate, suppose we have a variable named X and the number 2 is stored in that location. The program

```
100 LET X = 2
110 PRINT "X"
120 PRINT X
130 END
```

shows the difference between string and variable output. Line 110 prints out the character X since X is enclosed in quotation marks. Line 120 prints 2 since that is the number stored in location X.

The rule is clear. Any characters contained within quotation marks are called strings. Strings are printed out exactly as listed. The computer does not attempt to analyze or detect what is in the strings. If a variable in a PRINT statement is not contained within quotes, the computer prints out the numerical value of that variable.

It is possible to do computation within a PRINT statement. Thus

```
100 PRINT A+B+C,D
```

will cause the computer to print out the sum of the numbers stored in A, B, and C, then the number stored in D. Of course, the variables A, B, C, and D would have to be previously defined.

Spacing the Printout

BASIC has a "built-in" standard spacing mechanism that prints five numbers spaced equally on one line. (Note: Your computer may have fewer than five columns in this standard spacing. We will assume though, that there are five zones.) This standard spacing is used by the computer when quantities in a PRINT statement are separated by commas. The comma signals the computer to move to the next print position on the line. If the computer is already at the fifth position on a line and encounters a comma in a PRINT statement, it does a carriage return and prints the number on the first position on the next line. Thus

```
100 PRINT A,B,C,D,E,F
```

Input, Output, and Simple Applications 79

would cause the numerical values of A, B, C, D, and E to be printed evenly spaced across a line in the five standard positions. The numerical value of F would be printed below the value of A on the next line.

Commas in PRINT statements produce 5 columns per line.

Another type of spacing is produced by the semicolon between variables such as

```
100 PRINT A;B;C
```

The semicolon produces closer spacing than the standard spacing obtained with the comma. However, the spacing is not always uniform, since numbers may be typed out in different formats. We will let it go with the statement that

```
100 PRINT A;B
```

produces closer spacing of output than

```
100 PRINT A,B
```

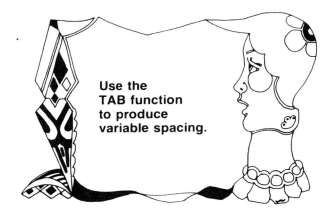

Use the TAB function to produce variable spacing.

Finally, we can control the spacing on a line in great detail by using the TAB function in PRINT statements. The TAB function works the same way as a tabulator setting on a typewriter. There are seventy-two tab positions available on most terminals. Some of the wide terminals may have more, but seventy-two is the usual number.

The statement

```
100 PRINT TAB(15);A;TAB(32);B
```

signals the computer to space over to the fifteenth printing position, print the numerical value of A, space over to the thirty-second printing position, and finally print the numerical value of B. It is also possible to have a variable tab setting that is controlled by the computer:

```
100 PRINT TAB(X);A
```

Here the computer must first look up the value of X, then space over to the printing position determined by the largest integer in X (for example, if X = 23.1435, the computer will space over to the twenty-third printing position), then print out the numerical value of A.

One final comment about the PRINT statement. We can produce vertical spacing in the output by using an empty PRINT statment as follows:

```
100 PRINT
```

Input, Output, and Simple Applications **81**

The computer looks for the quantity to be printed and finds none. It then looks for punctuation, and finding none, orders a carriage return and advances the paper one line. If we wanted two or three empty lines in the printout, we can obtain the spacing by using as many empty PRINT statements as desired.

The REMARK Statement

The REM (stands for "remark") statement is quite different from the statements we have seen previously. As soon as the computer senses the characters REM following the line number, it ignores the balance of the statement and goes on to the next line. What, then, is the purpose of the REM statement if the computer pays no attention to it? The REM statement is a way of providing information for the benefit of the programmer or someone reading the program. This information makes it much easier to follow what is taking place in the program. The wise programmer will use REM statements liberally.

To illustrate the use of the REM statements, two programs will be presented. They both will produce identical results, but the second uses REM statements to describe what is happening in the program. You can be the judge of which program is easier to follow.

1. No REM statements:

```
100 INPUT A,B,C,D
110 LET X = (A+B+C+D)/4
120 PRINT X
130 END
```

2. With REM statements:

```
100 REM COMPUTE THE AVERAGE OF FOUR NUMBERS
110 REM INPUT THE FOUR NUMBERS
120 INPUT A,B,C,D
130 REM COMPUTE THE AVERAGE
140 LET X = (A+B+C+D)/4
150 REM PRINT OUT THE AVERAGE
160 PRINT X
170 END
```

4-4 PROGRAM EXAMPLES

As we said, we will spend progressively more time writing and debugging programs. The examples chosen for this chapter are very simple but illustrate the ideas we have been discussing. Study each example carefully until you are certain that you understand all the details. You might want to enter the programs into the computer and execute them to verify that they work as intended.

Example 1 - Unit Prices

Our problem is to write a program to compute unit prices on supermarket items. We will let T stand for the total price, N for the number of items, and U for the unit price. We can compute the unit price with the following relationship:

$$U = T/N$$

As an example, suppose that a case of twelve large cans of fruit juice costs $6.96. The unit cost per can would then be

$$U = 6.96/12 = \$0.58$$

Input, Output, and Simple Applications   83

We want the program to be designed so that when executed it will produce the following output:

```
WHAT IS THE TOTAL PRICE? (You enter value of T)
WHAT IS THE NUMBER OF ITEMS? (You enter value of N)
UNIT PRICE IS (Computer types out value of U)
```

Now we will break this example apart to see how the program is related to what we want to see in the output.

```
WHAT IS THE TOTAL PRICE? (Entry of T)
      100                        200

WHAT IS THE NUMBER OF ITEMS ? (Entry of N)
      300                           400

500: Compute unit price.

UNIT PRICE IS (Output of U)
      600          700
```

We will write each line of the program so that the numbers above will be the line numbers in the program. In line 100 we want the computer to type out the message indicated. This is done with a PRINT command.

```
100 PRINT "WHAT IS THE TOTAL PRICE ";
```

Note the semicolon outside the closing quotation marks. The reason for this is that we do not want to get a carriage return but instead want the printed line to hold there for the INPUT prompt. Line 200 should be an INPUT statement to call for the input of T.

```
200 INPUT T
```

The message in line 300 requires a PRINT statement.

```
300 PRINT "WHAT IS THE NUMBER OF ITEMS ";
```

84 BASIC: A Hands-on Method

The input for the total number of items is handled the same as the total price.

```
400 INPUT N
```

Next we compute the unit price in line 500.

```
500 LET U = T/N
```

The next line is a message, followed by the unit price, and is handled with a PRINT statement.

```
600 PRINT "UNIT PRICE IS ";U
```

Finally we must have an END statement.

```
700 END
```

Now we pull the whole program together.

```
100 PRINT "WHAT IS THE TOTAL PRICE ";
200 INPUT T
300 PRINT "WHAT IS THE NUMBER OF ITEMS ";
400 INPUT N
500 LET U = T/N
600 PRINT "UNIT PRICE IS ";U
700 END
```

Study the program to make sure you see the purpose of each line as related to the original statement of the problem.

Input, Output, and Simple Applications **85**

Example 2 – Converting Temperature

The relationship between temperature measured in degrees Fahrenheit and in degrees Celsius is

$$C = (5/9)(F-32)$$

Let C stand for degrees Celcius and F stand for degrees Fahrenheit. If, for example, F is 212, then C is determined to be

$$C = (5/9)(212-32) = 100$$

As in the first example, we will write the program after seeing how we want the ouput to appear. Let's suppose that if we execute the desired program, we want to see the following:

```
INPUT NO. OF DEGREES F
? (You enter value of F)
(Computer types back F) DEGREES F IS (answer) DEGREES C
```

Again we will split the output up into parts that will be generated by the lines in the program:

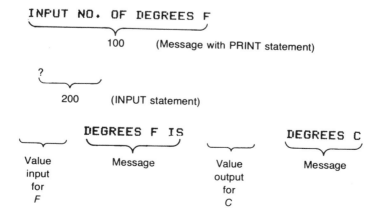

86 BASIC: A Hands-on Method

All this will be done in line 400. The corresponding program is

```
100 PRINT "INPUT NO. OF DEGREES F "
200 INPUT F
300 LET C = (5/9)*(F-32)
400 PRINT F;" DEGREES F IS ";C;" DEGREES C"
500 END
```

This program is a bit different from the first example. In line 100 there is no punctuation following the string. Thus the INPUT prompt generated by the INPUT statement in line 200 will be printed on the line following the initial string. The PRINT statement in line 400 prints out (1) the value of F, (2) a string, (3) the value of C, and (4) a second string. The semicolons in line 400 are used to set off the variables and strings in the PRINT statements.

Example 3 - Sum and Product of Numbers

The final example in this chapter will be concerned with the computation of the sum and product of two numbers. Again we will write the program to get the desired output. In this case, when the program is executed, we want to see

```
INPUT A ? (You enter value of A)
INPUT B ? (You enter value of B)
SUM OF A AND B IS (Computer prints out sum)
PRODUCT OF A AND B IS (Computer prints out product)
INPUT A ? (You enter value of A)
        (etc.)
```

Since we broke the first two examples apart in great detail, we can proceed more rapidly with this problem. The first line of the desired output can be handled by the following two statements:

```
100 PRINT "INPUT A ";
110 INPUT A
```

Note carefully that the message printed out in line 100 is window dressing for the program and has nothing to do with the actual calculations. The input instruction that is important to the computer is in line 110. We generate the second line of desired output as follows:

```
120 PRINT "INPUT B ";
130 INPUT B
```

The sum and product of the two numbers is printed out as follows:

```
140 PRINT "SUM OF A AND B IS ";A+B
150 PRINT "PRODUCT OF A AND B IS ";A*B
```

The spacing between the output of the original set of numbers and that obtained when the program loops back, as well as the looping instructions, can be obtained with three statements.

```
160 PRINT
170 PRINT
180 GOTO 100
```

Of course, the final line must be the END statement.

```
190 END
```

The whole program is listed below.

```
100 PRINT "INPUT A ";
110 INPUT A
120 PRINT "INPUT B ";
130 INPUT B
140 PRINT "SUM OF A AND B IS ";A+B
150 PRINT "PRODUCT OF A AND B IS ";A*B
160 PRINT
170 PRINT
180 GOTO 100
190 END
```

As structured, the program will keep looping back until we jump the program out of the INPUT loop. We could have computed the sum and product of the two numbers in separate lines, as in the following version of the same program:

```
100 PRINT "INPUT A ";
110 INPUT A
120 PRINT "INPUT B ";
130 INPUT B
140 LET S = A+B
150 PRINT "SUM OF A AND B IS ";S
160 LET P= A*B
170 PRINT "PRODUCT OF A AND B IS ";P
180 PRINT
190 PRINT
200 GOTO 100
210 END
```

4-5 PROBLEMS

1. Write a program that will read the four numbers 10, 9, 1, and 2 from a DATA statement, putting the numbers in A, B, C, and D, respectively. Add the first two numbers putting the sum in S. Then compute the product of the last two numbers, putting the result in P. Print out the value of S and P on the same line.

2. Write a program that will call for the input of four numbers, then print back the numbers in reverse order. For example, if you type in 5, 2, 11, 12, the computer should type back 12, 11, 2, 5. The program must work for any set of four numbers that you decide to type in. Oh yes, you can use only three lines in your program.

3. Write a program to read variables A, B, C, and D from numbers of your choice in a DATA statement. Print out the numbers vertically with B below A, C below B, and D below C.

4. What will be output if we execute the following program?

```
100 READ X,Y,Z
110 DATA 2,5,3
120 LET T = X*Y+Z
130 LET S = Y^2
140 PRINT T,S
150 END
```

5. What is wrong with this program?

```
100 LET A = 2
110 READ B
120 LET A = A+C/B
130 DATA 3
140 PRINT A
150 END
```

6. Explain in your own words what the following program does.

```
100 INPUT A,B
110 LET S = A+B
120 LET T = A-B
130 LET U = A*B
140 PRINT S,T,U
150 END
```

7. One of the ratios used to judge the health of a business is the acid-test ratio. The acid-test ratio is the sum of cash, marketable securities, and receivables, the sum divided by current liabilities. Write a program to call for the input of the necessary quantities, then compute and output the acid-test ratio.

8. Write a program to count and print out by fives beginning with 0. The first few numbers will be 0, 5, 10, 15, and so on. Interrupt the program manually when forty or fifty numbers have been printed out.

9. The intended output of the program below is 1, 3, 5, 7, 9, and so forth. The program below has an error. What is wrong?

```
100 LET A = 1
110 PRINT A;
120 LET A = A+2
130 GOTO 100
140 END
```

10. If an object is dropped near the surface of the earth, the distance it will fall in a given time can be determined by

$$S = 16T^2$$

where S is the distance fallen (in feet) and T is the time of fall in seconds. Write a program that when executed will produce the following output:

```
TIME OF FALL (SEC) ? (You enter T)
OBJECT FALLS (Computer types out S) FEET
```

11. The volume of a box can be computed as

$$V = LWH$$

where L, W, H are the length, width and height, respectively. If these are al measured in centimeters, for example, the volume will be in cubic centimeters. We want a program that will produce the following output when executed:

```
LENGTH (CM) ? (You enter L)
WIDTH (CM) ? (You enter W)
HEIGHT (CM) ? (You enter H)
VOLUME IS (Computer types out V) CUBIC CM.
```

The program below is incorrect and will not produce the output called for above. What is wrong?

```
100 PRINT "LENGTH (CM)";L
110 PRINT "WIDTH (CM)";W
120 PRINT "HEIGHT (CM)";H
130 INPUT L,W,H
140 LET V = L*W*H
150 PRINT "VOLUME IS"
160 PRINT V
170 PRINT "CUBIC CM."
180 END
```

Input, Output, and Simple Applications **91**

12. In the program below two numbers, A and B, are called for in the INPUT statement. The problem is to supply the missing statements so that when A and B are printed out, the values have been interchanged.

```
100 INPUT A,B
110
120
130
140 PRINT A,B
150 END
```

13. Suppose the odometer on your car reads R1 miles when the gas tank is full. You drive until the odometer reading is R2, at which point G gallons of gasoline are required to fill the tank. The miles per gallon you got on the drive is

$$M = (R_2 - R_1)/G$$

Write a program to figure out the mileage for the following data:

R_1	R_2	G
21423	21493	5
05270	05504	13
65214	65559	11.5

14. Let's suppose you are writing a program to print out numbers on a form. Assume that there are three numbers to be handled and they are in a DATA statement. Write a program which will print the first number beginning 20 characters in from the left of the output device. Follow this with two blank lines. Print the second number beginning at character 10. Print a blank line followed by the third number beginning at character 15. Put any numbers you wish in the DATA statement and try out the program.

15. It is known that a DATA statement contains examination grades for a class of ten students. Write a program containing no more than four statements counting the DATA and END statement to compute and print out the class average. Try out the program on sample data of your choice.

16. There is an old tale of a wise man who invented the game of chess and as a reward asked to receive 1 grain of wheat on the first square of the chess board, 2 grains on the second, 4 grains on the third, 8 on the fourth, and so on. Write a program to print out the square number and the number of grains on that square. The program should involve a loop using a GOTO statement and should be interrupted at the keyboard when you have seen enough. How many grains of wheat will be on the 64th square? RUN the program and find out.

17. If compound interest is paid, the true annual interest rate is higher than the nominal rate which is quoted for the investment. The following BASIC formula computes this true annual interest rate:

$$T = ((1+R/(100*M))^M-1)*100$$

In this expression, T is the true annual interest rate in percent, R is the nominal interest rate in percent, and M is the number of times the investment is compounded per year. Write a program which will produce the following output when executed:

```
QUOTED INTEREST RATE (PERCENT)
? (type in at keyboard)
NUMBER OF TIMES COMPOUNDED PER YEAR
? (type in at keyboard)
TRUE ANNUAL INTEREST RATE IS
(computer types out answer)
```

18. Simple interest on an investment is computed according to the following rule:

$$I = (P)(R/100)(T/365)$$

where P is the principal invested at an annual interest rate R (expressed in percent) for a time T (expressed in days). Write a program which will generate the display shown below when executed.

```
WHAT IS THE PRINCIPAL
? (type in the principal at the keyboard)
WHAT IS THE ANNUAL INTEREST RATE (%)
? (type in the interest rate at the keyboard)
WHAT IS THE TERM IN DAYS
? (type in the term at the keyboard)
FOR AN INVESTMENT OF
(Computer types out the principal)
AT AN ANNUAL INTEREST RATE OF
(Computer types out the rate)
PERCENT INVESTED FOR
(Computer types out the term)
DAYS, THE INTEREST IS
(Computer types out the interest)
```

19. If an amount of money P is left to accumulate interest at a rate of I percent per year for N years, the money will grow to a total amount T given by

$$T = P*(1+I/100)^N$$

As an example, if P = $1000, I = 6 percent, and N = 5 years,

$$T = 1000*(1+6/100)^5 = 1338.23$$

Write a program that when executed will produce the following output:

```
INITIAL INVESTMENT ? (You enter P)
ANNUAL INTEREST RATE (%) ? (You enter I)
YEARS LEFT TO ACCRUE INTEREST ? (You enter N)
TOTAL VALUE IS (Computer types out T)
```

20. If an amount of money P is left to accumulate interest at I percent compounded J times per year for N years, the value of the investment will be

$$T = P*(1 + I/(100*J))^{(J*N)}$$

94 BASIC: A Hands-on Method

Write a program that will call for the input of P, I, J and N. Execute the program as needed to get the value of $1000 invested at 8 percent for 2 years compounded

a. Annually (J = 1),

b. Semiannually (J = 2)

c. Monthly (J = 12)

d. Weekly (J = 52)

e. Daily (J = 365)

If a savings and loan company makes a big advertising production about computing the interest every day instead of each week, should you get excited?

4-6 PRACTICE TEST

The practice test that follows is provided for you to check how well you have mastered the key points and objectives of the chapter. Check your answer against the key given at the end of the book.

1. What will be output if the following program is executed?

```
100 LET X = 1
110 PRINT X,
120 LET X = X+1
130 GOTO 110
140 END
```

_____

2. Describe three ways that numbers can be brought into a BASIC program.

_____

3. In a PRINT statement, what is a collection of characters between quotation marks called?

4. What is the purpose of the REM statement?

5. If there is a READ statement in a BASIC program, what other type of statement must also be present in the program?

6. What will happen if the following program is executed?

```
100 LET X = 3
110 LET Y = 4
120 PRINT "Y = ";X
130 END
```

7. How many standard print columns per line are provided for in BASIC when the print quantities are separated by commas?

8. How many DATA statements may there be in a program?

9. What is the TAB function used for in BASIC?

_____

10. What will happen if the following program is executed?

```
100 LET A = 1
110 LET B = 3
120 PRINT A,B
130 PRINT A;B
140 END
```

_____

11. The program

```
100 INPUT A,B
110 LET C = A+B
120 PRINT C
130 END
```

is executed, and in response to the INPUT prompt you type the numbers 10, 12, and 13. Describe exactly what will happen.

_____

12. Miles can be converted to kilometers by multiplying by 1.609. Thus, 10 miles equals 16.09 kilometers, and so on. Write a program that will produce the following printout when executed.

```
INPUT NO OF MILES? (You type in a number)
(Computer types your number) MILES EQUALS (Answer)
KILOMETERS
```

Decisions, Branching, and Applications

5-1 OBJECTIVES

The power of the computer rests in large part on its ability to make decisions about quanitites in programs. In this chapter we will explore this cabability and will go on with the continuing task of learning to program in BASIC, the objectives are as follows.

Making Decisions in Programs

Decisions made in programs can cause the computer to jump to line numbers out of numerical order. Such a transfer to a program line may be unconditional or may depend upon values of variables in the program. The effective use of these conditional and unconditional transfer statements makes simple programs produce powerful and useful results.

Program Applications

As in the previous chapter, we will go on learning how to apply the techniques we study to BASIC programs.

Finding Errors in Programs

Almost all programs have errors in them when first written. Troubleshooting programs is a vital skill that, like programming itself, can be learned.

97

98   BASIC: A Hands-on Method

5-2 DISCOVERY EXERCISES

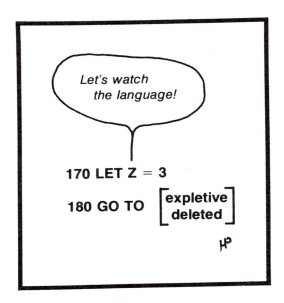

Computer Work

1. Sign on the computer and enter the following program:

```
100 LET X = 1
110 PRINT X
120 LET X = X+1
130 IF X < 5 THEN 110
140 END
```

The < symbol in line 130 means "less than"; thus, the statement translates as "If X is less than 5 then 110." Study the program carefully. What do you think will be printed out if you execute the program?

Decisions, Branching, and Applications **99**

Execute the program and record what did happen.

_____

2. Now type

                    100 LET X = 2

Display the program in work space. What will the output be now?

_____

Execute the program and write down what the computer printed out.

_____

3. Now let's make a few more changes in the program to see if you are following what is taking place. Type

                    100 LET X = 2
                    120 LET X = X+2

Display the program and study it carefully. What do you think the program will do now?

_____

BASIC: A Hands-on Method

Execute the program and see if you were right. Copy below what actually took place.

_____

4. We want to explore another idea in connection with the program you have in work space, but need to make some changes. If desired, you can modify the program to make it agree with the one below or clear out the program in work space and enter the one below.

```
100 LET X = 1
110 PRINT X
120 LET X = X+1
130 IF X >= 5 THEN 140
135 GOTO 110
140 END
```

Execute the program and record what happened.

_____

Compare the output recorded above to that you copied down in step 1. Is there any connection?

_____

5. In the program in step 4 there is an assertion stated in line 130. The assertion is X >= 5, which is read as "X is greater than or equal to 5." If for example, X had the numerical value 6, the assertion would be true. If X had the value 3, the assertion would be false. Now suppose we look at the program in step 4. If the program is executed, the computer starts with line 100, then goes to lines 110, 120, and 130. If the assertion in line 130 is true, which line number will the computer execute next?

_____

Decisions, Branching, and Applications **101**

6. Only two conditions have been used so far in the programs. They are

   < (Less than)

   > = (Greater than or equal to)

   How would you write the conditions for

   Greater than

   _____

   Less than or equal to

   _____

   Equal to

   _____

   Not equal to

   _____

   If you can fill in the blanks above without too much trouble, fine. If not, don't worry, as we will review everything later. The important thing now is how the IF THEN statement works.

7. Now on to some applications using IF THEN statements. Clear out the program in your work space and enter the following program:

```
100 PRINT "INPUT EITHER 1, 2, OR 3 ";
110 INPUT Y
```

```
120 IF Y = 1 THEN 150
130 IF Y = 2 THEN 170
140 IF Y = 3 THEN 190
150 PRINT "BLOOD"
160 GOTO 100
170 PRINT "SWEAT"
180 GOTO 100
190 PRINT "TEARS"
200 GOTO 100
210 END
```

Display the program and check that you have entered it correctly. Study the program briefly. Remember that when the program is executed and the computer types out the INPUT prompt, you are supposed to type in either, 1, 2, or 3. Which value of Y will let the computer reach line 120 in the program?

_____

Which value or values of Y will let the computer reach line 130?

_____

How about line 140?

_____

8. Suppose you wanted the computer to type out "SWEAT". What value of Y should be entered?

_____

See if you were right. Execute the program and enter the number you wrote down. What happened?

_____

Decisions, Branching, and Applications   **103**

9. What value of Y will cause the computer to type out BLOOD?

   _____

   How about making the computer type out TEARS?

   _____

   Check each of the responses you made above to see if you were right.

10. The program assumes that either 1, 2, or 3 will be typed in at the INPUT prompt. Think about the program a bit, then try to figure out what will happen if we type in 4 in response to the input prompt. What do you think will happen?

    _____

    Execute the program, type in 4 in response to the input prompt, and record below what happened.

    _____

    You can easily explain what happened in the program by considering what the computer does when it encounters an assertion in the IF THEN statement. Remember, if the assertion is true, the computer goes to the line number following the THEN. If the condition is false, the computer goes to the next higher line number. Now jump the computer out of the INPUT loop.

11. Sign off the computer and go on to the discussion of the objectives.

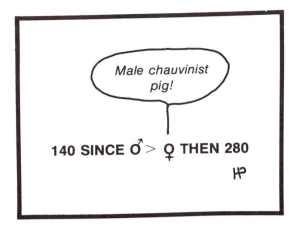

5-3 DISCUSSION

In this chapter we are concerned mainly with transfer statements, both conditional and unconditional, as well as their use in programs. Before getting to the programming, we will discuss each of the types of transfer statements.

Transfer without Conditions

From the very beginning of the book, we have been using unconditional transfer statements. The following program illustrates the use of the unconditional transfer statement:

```
100 LET Z = 2
110 PRINT Z
120 LET Z = 2*Z
130 GOTO 110
140 END
```

Recall that when ordered to execute a BASIC program, the computer goes to the statement with the lowest line number and then executes the statements in increasing line number order. The only way to interrupt this is with a transfer statement (or, as we will see in the next chapter, a loop command). In the program above, the computer would execute line number as follows: 100, 110, 120, 130, 110, 120, 130 110, 120, 130, and so on. The point is that the statement in line 130 causes the computer to jump back to line 110 instead of going to 140. Note that there are no conditions attached to the statement in line 130. This is why the GO TO statement is known as an unconditional transfer statement. It is also clear that the GO TO statement in this case puts the program into a loop and there is no way out. The only way we can get the computer out of the loop is to interrupt the program from the keyboard while it is running.

To sum up, if at some point in a program you want the computer to jump to another line without any conditions attached, use the GO TO statement. However, be careful that you don't get the program "hung up" in a loop.

Transfer on Conditions

By now you have most likely established the connection between the IF THEN statements you met in the computer work and the notion of the conditional transfer statement. All conditional transfer statements have the same form. A description of this form and a sample IF THEN statement are given below:

   Line # IF <(relation)> <(condition)> <(relation)> THEN Line #

     240 IF 3*X-2 > Y-Z THEN 360

No matter what the assertion, all IF THEN statements have this same format. The IF and THEN as well as the two line numbers in the statement require no special explanation. However, the heart of the statement lies in the two expressions separated by the condition that forms the assertion. We must look at them very carefully.

106 BASIC: A Hands-on Method

In all the examples we have met so far with the exception of the one above, the relations have been either simple variables or constants. This is the type of assertion used in programs most often. Examples might be

```
100 IF U < 3 THEN 250
340 IF S > T THEN 220
```

There are instances, however, in which we might want to use more complicated expressions in the IF THEN statements. In the example following the description of the IF THEN statement, the first relation was

$$3*X-2$$

which is fine providing that X has a value. The second relation,

$$Y-Z$$

Decisions, Branching, and Applications 107

can also be used if Y and Z have values. To further illustrate what takes place in a program, suppose that X has the value 1, Y is 10, and Z is 4. The computer will translate the statement

240 IF 3*X-2 > Y-Z THEN 360

by first substituting the values of X, Y, and Z. This changes the statement to

240 IF 1 > 6 THEN 360

Sooner or later, all IF THEN statement come down to this form, in which the computer must judge whether an assertion established by two numbers and a condition is true or false. In this case, the assertion 1 > 6 is false. However, an assertion like 4 < 10 would be true. If the assertion is true, the computer will go to the line number following THEN. If the assertion is false, the computer will go to the next higher line number in the program.

IF THEN statements branch if true. If false, then next higher line number.

Several conditions may be used in the IF THEN statement. The conditions and their meaning are listed below.

Condition	Meaning
=	Equal to
<	Less than
>	Greater than
<=	Less than or equal to
>=	Greater than or equal to
<>	Not equal to

To sum up, the IF THEN statement is a branching or transfer statement that depends upon whether an assertion in the statement is true or false. If the condition is true, the computer transfers to the line number at the end of the IF THEN statement. If the assertion is false, the computer goes to the next higher line number in the program. With the use of IF THEN (or conditional) transfer statements, the computer can be branched anywhere we desire in a program. This ability, more than anything seen so far, begins to reveal the true power of the computer.

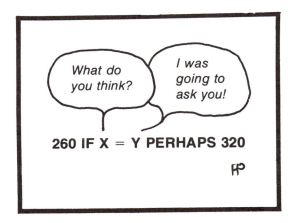

5-4 PROGRAM EXAMPLES

Up to this point our programs have suffered from a serious fault. On one hand, the program might involve repetition but there was no way to stop the process. On the other hand, the program stopped but often tended to be trivial. What we want is a way to have the program accomplish a useful task (which may involve repetition) and

Decisions, Branching, and Applications **109**

then shut itself off. The conditional transfer statements just learned provide a mechanism to do this. Now we will look at several programs that illustrate this capability.

Example 1 – Printout of Number Patterns

Our problem is to write a program that will print out the following number pattern when executed:

```
        2       3       4       5       6
        7       8       9      10      11
```

There are several characteristics of this pattern which we must think about when writing the program. The first number is 2, and succeeding numbers are spaced across in the standard spacing (five numbers to a line). Each number is 1 greater than the previous one. The last number printed out is 11, then the computer should stop.

Several solutions are possible. A program that's not the most elegant but would still work is

```
100 PRINT 2,3,4,5,6,7,8,9,10,11
110 END
```

You might check this program to see that is does in fact produce the correct number pattern. It also illustrates a very important concept. There is no such thing as the correct program. The only test that can be applied is "Does the program work?" Certainly some programs are cleverer or may accomplish the results more efficiently than others, but this is a separate issue. The beginner should be concerned with whether or not the BASIC program will produce the desired results rather than with questions of style.

Now back to the problem at hand. One way to approach the problem is to make the computer print out the first number in the pattern. We also want to organize the program so that only a single print statement is required. This will require that the program print out the value of a variable that will be changed as the program is executed. We can start our program with the following segment:

```
100 LET X = 2
110 PRINT X,
```

The value of X is set to 2, and this value is printed out in line 110. The comma causes the computer to space across to the next standard printing position. Now we must generate the next value to be printed out. Note that at any point in the number pattern, the next number is just 1 more than the present number. This can be done with

$$120 \text{ LET } X = X+1$$

Now all that remains is to make a decision about whether to loop back to the print statement or to stop. As long as X is less than or equal to 11, we want to loop back. We can do this with a conditional transfer statement.

$$130 \text{ IF } X <= 11 \text{ THEN } 110$$

The program is finished with an END statement.

$$140 \text{ END}$$

The complete program is

```
100 LET X = 2
110 PRINT X,
120 LET X = X+1
130 IF X <= 11 THEN 110
140 END
```

This program is a simple one and has little practical value other than to illustrate how a conditional transfer statement can get us out of a program at the proper time.

Example 2 – Automobile License Fees

Let's assume that in an attempt to force consumers to use lower-horsepower cars and conserve energy, the state adopts a set of progressive annual license fees

Decisions, Branching, and Applications 111

based upon the power rating of the car. The criteria and fees are listed below.

Horsepower	License Fee
Up to 50 hp	$ 0
More than 50 but 100 hp or less	30
More than 100 but 200 hp or less	70
More than 200 but 300 hp or less	150
More than 300 hp	500

We want a program that will produce the following output when executed:

```
INPUT AUTO HP? (You type in horsepower)
LICENSE FEE IS (Computer types out fee)

INPUT AUTO HP? (You type in horsepower)
LICENSE FEE IS (Computer types out fee)

           (etc.)
```

Clearly, the only difficult part of the program will be to decide what the fee is. This decision-making process is made to order for the IF THEN statement. To get started we must provide for input of the power rating. We will use P to stand for the power rating of the car. The program can begin with

```
100 PRINT "INPUT AUTO HP ";
110 INPUT P
```

Now, we must work out a method to decide in which license category P lies. A logical way to do this would be to check upward from the low horsepower ratings. First, we can check whether P is 50 or less. If so, then we know the tax is 0.

```
120 IF P <= 50 THEN _____(Fee is 0)
```

The line number following THEN is missing for this reason. If the number in P is less than or equal to 50, we want the computer to jump to a statement that will assign the value 0 to the fee. The problem is that we don't know at this point what line number should be used for this statement. Consequently, we will leave it blank and will return later on and insert the proper value. The note at the right is there to remind us of what the fee is supposed to be if the assertion is true and the branch is taken.

If the assertion in line 120 is false, the computer will go to the next higher line number. In that case we want to check to see if P falls in the next higher category.

```
130 IF P <= 100 THEN _____(Fee is $30)
```

Again, we don't know what line number to use following the THEN but can fill it in later. There are three branch statements left to determine completely which category contains P. Now that the pattern is established, we can include them all at once.

```
140 IF P <= 200 THEN _____(Fee is $70)
150 IF P <= 300 THEN _____(Fee is $150)
160 IF P> 300 THEN _____(Fee is $500)
```

The program to this point is

```
100 PRINT "INPUT AUTO HP ";
110 INPUT P
120 IF P <= 50 THEN _____(Fee is 0)
130 IF P <= 100 THEN _____(Fee is $30)
140 IF P <= 200 THEN _____(Fee is $70)
150 IF P <= 300 THEN _____(Fee is $150)
160 IF P > 300 THEN _____(Fee is $500)
```

Now we can fill in the missing line number in line 120. Since the next line number in the program would be 170, we may as well use it.

```
100 PRINT "INPUT AUTO HP ";
110 INPUT P
120 IF P <= 50 THEN 170
130 IF P <= 110 THEN _____(Fee is $30)
140 IF P <= 200 THEN _____(Fee is $70)
150 IF P <= 300 THEN _____(Fee is $150)
160 IF P > 300 THEN _____(Fee is $500)
170 LET F = 0
180 GOTO _____(PRINT statement)
```

Again, in line 180 we have a missing line number. The reminder is that we want to transfer to a PRINT statement. If the assertion in line 120 is true, the computer jumps to line 170 and assigns the value 0 to F, which stands for the fee. We can go on filling in the missing numbers in lines 130, 140, 150, and 160 using the same pattern. The result is

```
100 PRINT "INPUT AUTO HP ";
110 INPUT P
120 IF P <= 50 THEN 170
130 IF P <= 100 THEN 190
140 IF P <= 200 THEN 210
150 IF P <= 300 THEN 230
160 IF P > 300 THEN 250
170 LET F = 0
180 GOTO _____(PRINT statement)
190 LET F = 30
200 GOTO _____(PRINT statement)
210 LET F = 70
220 GOTO _____(PRINT statement)
230 LET F = 150
240 GOTO _____(PRINT statement)
250 LET F = 500
```

The next line in the program would be 260, which we may as well use for the PRINT statement. The rest of the program follows easily. The complete program is given below.

```
100 PRINT "INPUT AUTO HP ";
110 INPUT P
120 IF P <= 50 THEN 170
130 IF P <= 100 THEN 190
140 IF P <= 200 THEN 210
150 IF P <= 300 THEN 230
160 IF P > 300 THEN 250
170 LET F = 0
180 GOTO 260
190 LET F = 30
200 GOTO 260
210 LET F = 70
220 GOTO 260
230 LET F = 150
240 GOTO 260
250 LET F = 500
260 PRINT "LICENSE FEE IS ";F
270 PRINT
280 GOTO 100
290 END
```

You may have noticed that the conditional transfer statement in line 160 is not necessary. To see why, consider each of the assertions in the IF THEN statements. If the assertion in line 120 is false, we know that P must be greater than 50. Likewise, if each of the following assertions are false, the computer goes to the next higher line number. In particular, suppose the computer reaches line 150 and determines that the assertion is false. This directs the computer to line 160, but then we know that P must be greater than 300 and can therefore print out the fee without any more testing. If we assign the license fee of $500 in line 160, the result is a slightly different program:

```
100 PRINT "INPUT AUTO HP ";
110 INPUT P
120 IF P <= 50 THEN 200
130 IF P <= 100 THEN 220
140 IF P <= 200 THEN 240
150 IF P <= 300 THEN 260
160 LET F = 500
170 PRINT "LICENSE FEE IS ";F
180 PRINT
190 GOTO 100
200 LET F = 0
210 GOTO 170
220 LET F = 30
230 GOTO 170
240 LET F = 70
250 GOTO 170
260 LET F = 150
270 GOTO 170
280 END
```

Both versions of the program will work equally well, and you may have your own version. How you prefer to handle the branches is a matter for you to decide. The only question is whether your program will work.

We have gone through this program in great detail because it often proves difficult for the beginner to write programs involving such search rules. You should study the program until you are convinced that it does accomplish what was desired. Also, try to remember to use the technique of leaving line numbers out when you do not know what they should be, then returning later to fill in the proper values. The comments at the right of the page in these cases will help you remember what you want to happen at that branch point in the program.

Example 3 – Averaging Numbers

Suppose we have numbers in a DATA statement which we wish to average. The problem is that we don't know in advance how many numbers there are. So we will

Decisions, Branching, and Applications 115

use the strategy of a flag variable to mark the end of the data. The flag will be a number that is very unlikely to occur in the data. We will use the number 9999 for our flag, but you could select one of your own choice if desired.

Here is the way it will work. The DATA statement will always appear as follows:

```
Line #    DATA (number),(number),....,(number),9999
```

The flag 9999 is put in the data after the last number to be averaged. In the program, each time we read a number from the DATA statement we must check to see if it is 9999. If not, we know that the number just read is part of the data to be averaged. If the number is 9999 we know we have read in all the data and can go on to the rest of the program.

An average is computed by dividing the sum of the numbers by the number of numbers. In our program we must compute both these quantities. We will use S to stand for the sum of the numbers and N for the number of numbers. When the program is executed, we do not know what these values will be, so we must set them equal to 0 and then develop their values as we read in numbers from the DATA statements.

The program begins by setting up the initial values of S and N.

```
100 LET S = 0
110 LET N = 0
```

Now we can read a number from the DATA statement and check for the flag value.

```
120 READ X
130 IF X = 9999 THEN _____ (Compute average)
```

We are using the method, introduced in the previous example, of leaving a line number blank in the conditional transfer statement until we know what it should be. In this case, if the assertion (X = 9999) is true then we know that all the numbers in the DATA statement have been processed and we are ready to compute the average. If the assertion is false, then the number just read must be part of the data and should be processed. This is done as follows:

```
140 LET S = S+X
150 LET N = N+1
```

In line 140, the value of X (the number just read) is added to the value in S. Remember that the sum of all the numbers to be averaged is being developed in S. In line 150, the number in N is incremented by 1 to record the fact that another number has been processed.

```
160 GOTO 120
```

Now we can fill in the missing number in line 130, since the next line number in the program would normally be 170. In line 170 we compute the average, which we will identify by A. If a typical DATA statement is included, the complete program is

```
100 LET S = 0
110 LET N = 0
120 READ X
130 IF X = 9999 THEN 170
140 LET S = S+X
150 LET N = N+1
160 GOTO 120
170 LET A = S/N
180 PRINT A
190 DATA 4,2,3,6,5,9999
200 END
```

Of course, we can have as many DATA statments as needed to hold the numbers to be averaged. Following the last number in the last DATA statement we put the flag 9999 to mark the end of the data. This gets us out the READ loop and lets us know when to go on to compute the average. The conditional transfer statement, coupled with the idea of a flag variable, gives us a powerful tool to use in programs.

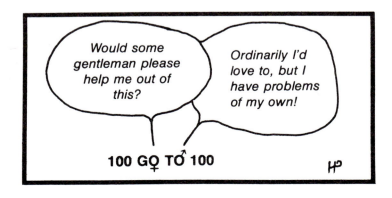

5-5 FINDING ERRORS IN PROGRAMS

The ability to look at a program and determine whether or not it will accomplish what it is supposed to do is certainly one of the most important skills a beginner can acquire. Probably more to the point, when a program is not doing what it is supposed to do, can you find out what is wrong and correct it? These abilities are strange in that until learned, they appear to be very difficult. However, once learned, the programmer usually has great difficulty understanding why everyone doesn't have the same abilities.

Two separate tasks are involved in troubleshooting programs. First, you must be able to translate a BASIC statement into what it means to the computer. Next, you must be able to trace a BASIC program, detailing each step and action as it takes place. We are now far enough into the task of learning about BASIC than we can profitably spend some time on troubleshooting programs. The time spent doing this is golden and will be paid back many times over in time saved in the future.

Translating BASIC Statements

We have been using several different types of BASIC statements. We want to review just what the computer does when it executes these statements. As an example, suppose the computer evaluates the statement

$$140 \ \text{LET} \ X = 3$$

This statement instructs the computer to set up a memory location, name it X and store a 3 in that location. Likewise

$$160 \ \text{LET} \ B = 0$$

causes the computer to name a memory location B and store a 0 in that location.

The situation is a bit more complicated with the following statement:

$$135 \ \text{LET} \ X = A+B-2$$

Now the computer is directed to get the numbers stored in A and B, add them together, subtract 2, and store the result in a location to be named X. This is all right provided that the computer can find memory locations named A and B. If these had not been set up prior to the statements being executed, the computer would search for the locations A and B, and, finding none, would signal and error and stop. On

118 BASIC: A Hands-on Method

some computers if the locations A and B could not be found, the computer will set up A and B with zeros in the locations. You must be careful about this since the zeros might produce results you didn't want!

What happens when the computer encounters a statement like

$$185 \text{ IF } M = N \text{ THEN } 240$$

which directs the computer to get the numbers in M and N and see if they are equal? If the numbers are equal, then the next line number to be executed would be 240. If not, the computer would go to the next higher line number. If the computer can't find locations M and N, it will signal an error and stop. Or, as pointed out above, if M and N are not defined, some computers may set up M and N with zero values. This would be particularly bad here since it would lead to an assertion that would always be true.

Now we want to use the knowledge of how to translate BASIC statements to locate any errors that may be in a program.

Tracing BASIC Programs

The program developed in Example 3 in the previous section will be a good one to use to learn how to troubleshoot. The program is given again below for your reference.

```
100 LET S = 0
110 LET N = 0
120 READ X
130 IF X = 9999 THEN 170
140 LET S = S+X
150 LET N = N+1
160 GOTO 120
170 LET A = S/N
180 PRINT A
190 DATA 4,2,3,6,5,9999
200 END
```

The job at hand now is to convince you that the best and most foolproof aid to programming is a blank sheet of paper! Used correctly, this "little dandy" programming aid will enable you to find all the errors in your programs and reveal how to correct them. This sounds like a big order for such a simple device as a blank sheet of paper, but it's true! Now let's find out how to do it.

First, copy the program on a lined sheet of paper and follow through our discussion using this copy. Place a blank sheet of paper over everything except the first line of the program

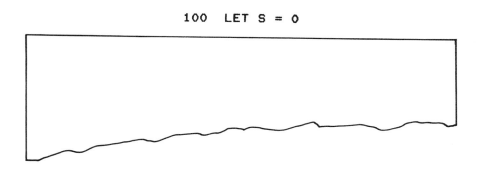

100   LET S = 0

Now we translate the statement, which tells the computer to set up a memory location called S, and store a 0 there. We will use our blank sheet of paper to keep track of what is in the computer memory. So we write down an S and underneath place a 0.

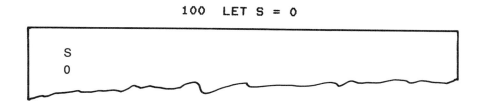

100   LET S = 0

S
0

This finishes the first line in the program. Slide the sheet of paper down to reveal the next line and do what is directed. Remember that you are playing the part of the computer and are using the sheet of paper to record what is in the computer memory as well as to let you see only one line of the program at a time.

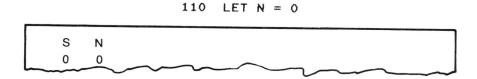

110   LET N = 0

S   N
0   0

Now on to line 120.

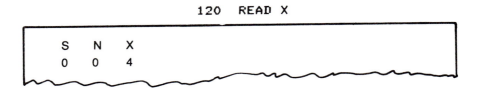

Here the computer is instucted to read a number from the DATA statement in the program, which in this case is 4. The 4 is stored in a location called X.

Let's pause to review what we are doing. We are going through the program one line at a time, writing down what the computer is directed to do. Since we haven't yet met any transfer statements, we simply evaluate a statement, then go on to the next higher numbered statement. Now on to line 130.

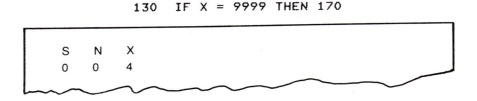

The assertion in line 130 (X = 9999) is evaluated using the value of X that appears on the paper. Since at this point in the program, X, has the value 4, the assertion (4 = 9999) is false. Consequently, instead of going to 170 we drop through to the next line in the program,

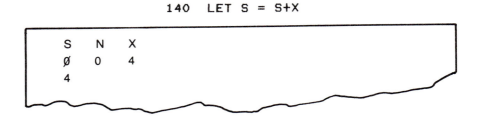

We get the number in S (0) and the number in X (4), add them together, and store the sum of 4 in S. Note that this destroys the previous value stored in S. We will simply line out any destroyed value to indicate that it has been lost. At any point in our trace of the program, the value of a variable will be the last number written down in that column. Now the computer goes to line 150.

Decisions, Branching, and Applications **121**

150   LET N = N+1

```
S    N    X
Ø    Ø    4
4    1
```

Here the number 1 was added to the 0 in N, and the sum was then stored in N, destroying the 0 stored there previously. Line 160 directs the computer to go back to the READ statement in line 120. Then the whole process starts again. We stay in this loop until all the data are read in and processed. If you keep tracing the program until the flag 9999 is read into X, your sheet of paper should look as follows:

130   IF X = 9999 THEN 170

```
S     N     X
Ø     Ø     4
4     1     2
6     2     3
9     3     6
15    4     5
20    5     9999
```

Since the value of X is now 9999, the assertion (X = 9999) is true and the computer is branched to line 170,

170   LET A = S/N

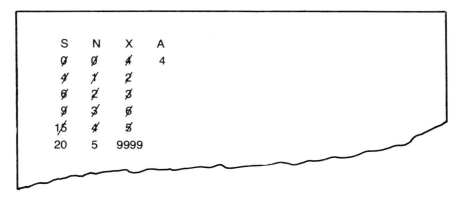

The computer sets up a location called A, divides the number in S by the number in N, and stores the result in A. Finally, the computer is directed in line 180 to print out the value stored in A. Our trace has revealed that the computer is doing what we intended and producing the correct results.

Now let's look at a program that is incorrect and use the tracing technique to find out what is wrong. The program is supposed to compute the sum of numbers typed in at the terminal. Each time the computer types out an INPUT prompt, we type in one number. When all the numbers are in, we type in 11111 as a flag to indicate that we are through. The computer is then supposed to type out the sum of the numbers entered prior to the flag. The program below is incorrect.

```
100 LET S = 0
110 INPUT Y
120 IF Y = 11111 THEN 150
130 LET S = S+Y
140 GOTO 100
150 PRINT S
160 END
```

We will use our little dandy programming aid to find out what is wrong. To test the program we will assume that the following sequence of numbers is typed in as the INPUT prompts are displayed:

3,1,6,5,11111

The sum of the numbers before the flag is 15. So we know in advance that this is what the computer should print out.

We begin with the blank sheet of paper and the first line of the program,

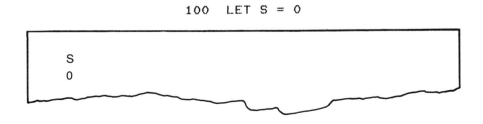

Then

Decisions, Branching, and Applications   **123**

110   INPUT Y

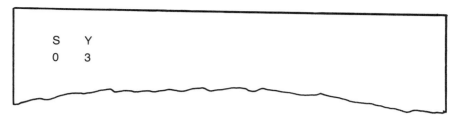

Since Y is not 11111 we go to line 130,

130   LET S = S+Y

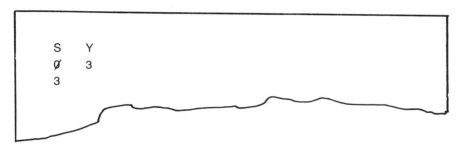

After line 130 we transfer back to line 100,

100   LET S = 0

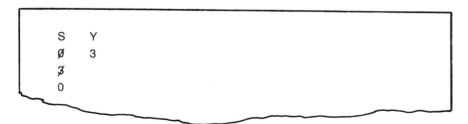

If you follow the program until the flag 11111 is entered, your sheet of paper should look as follows:

120   IF Y = 11111 THEN 150

```
S           Y
0           0
0           1
0           0
1           0
0           11111
0
0
0
0
```

Since at this point, Y contains the value of 11111, the computer jumps to line 150, which calls for the number S to be printed out. But the number in S is 0, which is clearly incorrect. If you followed through, tracing the program and writing down all the steps, then you have probably already discovered what is wrong. The error is in the unconditional transfer statement in line 140. With the transfer to line 100, the value in S (which is supposed to contain the sum of the numbers as they are typed in) is set equal to 0 each time a number is entered. The problem is easily corrected by changing the line to

GO TO 110

Take the time to learn how to trace programs. If you don't, much time will be lost later on in speculation about what is wrong in your programs.

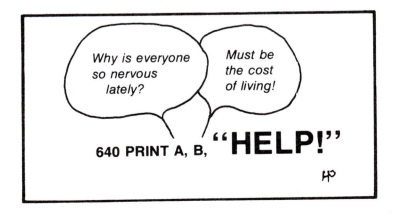

5-6 PROBLEMS

1. Write a BASIC program to call for the input of two numbers. Then print out the larger.

2. Write a BASIC program to READ three numbers from a DATA statement and then print out the smallest.

3. Write a program to compute and print out the sum of all the whole numbers between 1 and 100 inclusive.

4. What will happen if the following program is executed. Describe in your own words.

```
100 LET S = 0
110 LET X = 1
120 LET S = S+X
130 LET X = X+2
140 IF X < 100 THEN 120
150 PRINT S
160 END
```

5. In Example 3 in this chapter, substitute the following DATA statement:

```
190 DATA 4,2,3,6,5,1111
```

Trace the program by hand and write down what will be output if the program is executed.

6. Trace the program below by hand using the inputs indicated. In each case, find what will be printed out.

   a. 1, 2, 3

   b. 3, 2, 1

   c. 2, 2, 2

   d. 3, 1, 3

```
100 INPUT A,B,C
110 IF A < B THEN 150
```

```
120 IF B >= C THEN 170
130 LET D = A+B+C
140 GOTO 180
150 LET D = A*B-C
160 GOTO 180
170 LET D = A+B*C
180 PRINT D
190 END
```

7. Suppose you are given a DATA statement that contains a list of numbers of unknown length. However, the end of the list is marked with the flag variable 9999. Write a BASIC program to compute and print out the sum of the numbers in the list between −10 and +10 inclusive.

8. Usually there is a different mark up for supermarkets depending upon the unit cost of the item. Suppose this mark up is based on the following schedule:

Unit Cost	Mark up
0 to $1.00	20%
$1.01 to $2.00	10%
over $2.00	5%

The unit cost is determined by dividing the case price by the number of items in the case. Write a program to compute label price which is unit cost plus mark up. Arrange for prompts and input any way you desire.

9. Suppose you agree to work for one cent the first day, two cents the second, four cents the third, eight cents the fourth and so on. If there are 22 working days in a month, what will your wages (in dollars) be?

10. Write a program to find the average of all the positive numbers in a list whose end is marked with the flag 9999. The list of numbers is to be typed in at the terminal at run time.

11. Trace the following program and determine what will be output. Can you describe what the program does?

```
100 READ N
110 LET L = 1
120 LET C = 1
130 READ X
140 LET C = C + 1
```

```
150 IF X < L THEN 170
160 LET L = X
170 IF C < N THEN 130
180 PRINT L
190 DATA 10
200 DATA 5,83,17,3,47
210 DATA 25,16,41,51,7
220 END
```

12. The following program is intended to find the average of N numbers typed in at the terminal. As it stands the program is incorrect. What's wrong?

```
100 PRINT "HOW MANY NUMBERS"
110 INPUT N
120 LET S = 0
130 LET C = 1
140 PRINT "TYPE IN A NUMBER";
150 INPUT X
160 LET S = S + X
170 LET C = C + 1
180 IF C < N THEN 140
190 LET A = S/N
200 PRINT "THE AVERAGE IS"; A
210 END
```

13. The discounted price of an item can be computed by

$$D = L*(1 - R/100)$$

where L is the purchase price and R is the discount rate in percent. Write a program that will produce the following output when executed:

```
LIST PRICE ($)? (You type in price)
DISCOUNT RATE (%)? (You type in rate)
DISCOUNTED PRICE IS
(Computer types out price) DOLLARS
```

14. There is an interesting sequence of numbers called the Fibonacci numbers. The set begins with 0, 1. Then each succeeding number in the sequence is the sum of the two previous ones. Thus, the Fibonacci sequence is

$$0, 1, 1, 2, 3, 5, 8, \ldots$$

Write a BASIC program to compute and print out the first twenty numbers in the Fibonacii sequence.

15. Write a program to accept the input of two numbers. If both the numbers are greater than or equal to 10, print out their sum. If both the numbers are less than 10, print out their product. If one number is greater than or equal to 10 and the other is less than 10, print out the difference between the largest and smallest.

16. An instructor decides to award letter grades on an examination as follows:

```
         90-100          A
         80- 89          B
         60- 79          C
         50- 59          D
          0- 49          F
```

Write a program to produce the following output when executed:

```
INPUT EXAM GRADE ?(You type in numerical grade)
YOUR GRADE IS (Computer types out A, B, C, D,
or F)
```

17. If you use 8 percent more electricity each year, in nine years your consumption will double. Thus your doubling time is nine years. It turns out that there is an interesting rule called the "rule of seventy-two" that can be used to compute doubling times. If a quantity grows by R percent in a single period of time, then the number of periods for the quantity to double is given approximately by 72/R. This is the rule of seventy-two. We can compute the growth of a process directly on the computer. In a single growth period, a quantity Q grows according to the relation

$$Q_{new} = Q_{old}(1 + R/100)$$

Thus we can keep track of the growth by repeated use of the relation above. When Q is twice the original value, the corresponding number of growth periods would be the doubling time. Using this approach, write a program that will produce the following output when executed:

```
GROWTH RATE (%) ? (You type in R)
NUMBER OF GROWTH PERIODS TO DOUBLE IS
(Computer types answer)
```

Use the program to check out the accuracy of the rule of seventy-two for many different growth rates.

18. A set of integers (whole numbers) is chosen at random from the set 1, 2, 3, 4 and put in a DATA statement. The end of the set is marked with the flag 9999. Write a BASIC program that will compute and print out the number of 1s, 2s, 3s, and 4s in the set. Test your program on the following DATA statement:

```
DATA 3,1,2,1,4,4,1,2,2,2,3,9999
```

19. Consider the series

$$1 + 1/2 + 1/3 + 1/4 + \ldots$$

Write a program to find the sum of the first N terms. Use this to find the sum of the first 10, 100, and 1000 terms. Based on these results what do you think the sum would be if we let the series run on forever.

5-7 PRACTICE TEST

Check your progress with the following practice test. The answers are in the key at the end of the book.

1. What will be output if the following program is executed?

```
100 LET Y = 3
110 LET X = 2*Y
120 PRINT X
130 LET Y = Y+2
140 IF Y <= 10 THEN 110
150 END
```

2. What will be output if the following program is executed?

```
100 READ X
110 DATA 1,2,3
120 IF X < 2 THEN 160
130 IF X = 2 THEN 150
140 PRINT "GOOD"
150 PRINT "BETTER"
160 PRINT "BEST"
170 PRINT
180 GOTO 100
190 END
```

3. Suppose that you decide to buy a number of widgets. The manufacturer is pushing sales so will give reduced prices for quantity purchases. The price detail is as follows:

# Purchased	Price per Widget
20 or less	$2.00
21 to 50	1.80
51 or more	1.50

Write a program that will produce the following output when executed:

```
HOW MANY WIDGETS ? (You type in purchase quantity)
PRICE PER WIDGET IS (Computer types out unit price)
TOTAL COST OF ORDER IS (Computer types out total)
```

Then keep looping back through the program.

4. Write a program that will print out the number pattern shown below and then stop.

```
   0      5     10     15     20
  25     30     35     40     45
                etc.

 150    155    160    165    170
```

5. If you get a ticket for speeding, your fine is based on how much you exceeded the speed limit. Suppose the fine is computed as follows:

Amount over Limit	Fine
1–10 mi/h	$ 5
11–20	10
21–30	20
31–40	40
41 or more	80

Write a BASIC program that will produce the following output when executed:

```
WHAT WAS SPEED LIMIT ? (You type in)
SPEED ARRESTED AT ? (You type in)
FINE IS (Computer types out fine) DOLLARS
```

Looping and Functions

6-1 OBJECTIVES

In this chapter we will learn about two interesting characteristics of BASIC which will provide new and powerful programming capability. The objectives are as follows.

Built-in Looping

We have already learned how to loop programs using either the unconditional or conditional transfer statements. BASIC has special statements to take care of looping automatically. These statements simplify the programming task and provide flexibility in programs.

Built-in Functions

BASIC contains a number of built-in functions that can be called on to perform specific tasks. We will look at some of the simpler of these functions that involve numerical computations and see how they can be used to advantage in BASIC programs. In chapter eight we will look at functions that involve strings of characters.

Program Applications

We will continue with activities designed to draw you into programming. Remember that the overall objective of the book is to teach you how to write BASIC language programs.

134 BASIC: A Hands-on Method

6-2 DISCOVERY EXERCISES

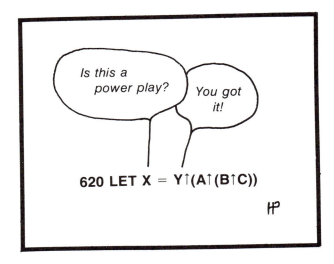

Computer Work

1. Sign on the computer and enter the following program:

```
100 LET Y = 10
110 PRINT Y,
120 LET Y = Y+5
130 IF Y <= 50 THEN 110
140 END
```

Study the program and then execute it. Record what happened.

_____

Which statement in the program determines the difference in the numbers that were typed out?

_____

Looping and Functions

2. Clear out the program in your work space. Now enter the following program:

```
100 FOR Y = 10 TO 50 STEP 5
110 PRINT Y,
120 NEXT Y
130 END
```

Execute the program and record what happened.

_____

Compare the output to that obtained from the program in step 1.

3. Since the two programs just executed produce the same output, it is reasonable to assume that the statements must be related in some way. Type

```
100 FOR Y = 10 TO 50 STEP 10
```

Display the program in your work space and study it. What do you think will happen if we execute this program?

_____

See if you were right. Execute the program and record the results below.

_____

4. Now let's try a few different ideas out on the program. Type

```
100 FOR Y = 0 TO 5 STEP 1
```

Display the program. What do you think this program will do?

_____

Execute the program and write down the output below.

_____

5. Now type

```
100 FOR Y = 0 TO 5
```

Display the program. What do you think this program will do?

_____

Execute the program and record what happened.

_____

Now compare line 100 in the program just executed with line 100 in the program in step 4. If the difference between the numbers to be printed out is 1, is the STEP part of the statement necessary?

_____

6. Let's try a different tactic. Type

Looping and Functions

```
100 FOR Y = 20 TO 10 STEP -2
```

Display the program and study it. What do you think this program will do?

_____

Execute the program and record the output.

_____

7. All right, now type

```
100 FOR Y = 10 TO 20 STEP -2
```

Display the program. What do you think will happen now if we execute the program?

_____

Execute the program and write down what happened.

_____

What we have done here is to lead you into a potential trap in BASIC. What seems to be the problem?

_____

8. So far the step sizes in the FOR NEXT statements have worked out without any problem. Let's try a new step size that might not come out even when compared to the limits in the FOR NEXT statement. Type

    100 FOR Y = 2 TO 9 STEP 3

    Display the program. Write down what you think will be printed out.

    _____

    Execute the program and record what happened.

    _____

9. We will go on now to some more involved situations involving FOR NEXT statements. Clear out the program in your work space and enter the following program:

    100 FOR X = 1 TO 3
    110 FOR Y = 1 TO 4
    120 PRINT X,Y
    130 NEXT Y
    140 NEXT X
    150 END

    Execute the program and record the output.

    _____

10. Now type

    100 FOR X = 1 TO 2

Execute this new program and record the output.

_____

Compare the two number patterns you have just obtained. Can you see the connection between the patterns and the limits in the FOR NEXT statements?

_____

11. Let's modify the program a bit more. Type

>   100 FOR X = 1 TO 3
>   110 FOR Y = 1 TO 2

Display this program and study it. What do you think will be output if it is executed?

_____

Try it and see if you were right.

_____

12. One more time. Type

>   100 FOR X = 1 TO 2
>   110 FOR Y = 1 TO 2

Display the program and write down what you think will be typed out when the program is executed.

_____

Execute the program and record the results below.

_____

On the listing of the program just executed, draw a line from the line number of the FOR X statement to the line number of the NEXT X statement. Do the same thing for the FOR Y and the NEXT Y statements. Do these lines cross?

_____

13. Now type

```
100 FOR Y = 1 TO 2
110 FOR X = 1 TO 2
```

Display the program. What do you think will be output by this program?

_____

Execute the program and record what happened.

_____

On the listing of this program, connect the FOR X and and NEXT X line numbers with a line just as you did in step 12. Do the same thing for the FOR Y and the NEXT Y statements. Do these lines cross? Compare with the same situation in step 12.

_____

Does this suggest a way to avoid getting into trouble using more than one FOR NEXT combination in a single program?

_____

14. In Chapter 4 we experimented with the TAB function to get variable spacing in the output. Now that we have the FOR NEXT statements at our disposal, let's go back to the TAB function. Clear out the program in your work space and enter the following program:

```
100 FOR X = 1 TO 5
110 PRINT TAB(X);
120 FOR Y = X TO 5
130 PRINT "Y";
140 NEXT Y
150 PRINT
160 NEXT X
170 END
```

Take a few moments to trace the program using the technique developed in the last chapter. Be sure to take the program step by step and write down all the values of the variables in the program as they occur. What output do you think the program will produce?

_____

See if you were right. Execute the program and record the output below.

_____

15. Clear out the program in your work space. Enter the program below.

```
100 INPUT A
110 LET B = SQR(A)
120 PRINT B
130 GOTO 100
140 END
```

Execute the program and at the INPUT prompt, type 4. What happened?

___

Now type in 9 and record the results.

___

One more time. Type in 25. What happened?

___

Finally, type in 10. What happened?

___

All right, what happens to A in the expression SQR(A) in line 110 of the program? In other words, what does SQR do?

___

16. Jump the computer out of the input loop. Type

```
110 LET B = INT(A)
```

Execute the program for the following values of A. In each case, record the output of the program.

A	Output
1	_____
3.4	_____
256.78	_____
0	_____
−1	_____
−2.3	_____

Examine the output you have recorded above and compare each number with the corresponding value of A that you typed in. What does the INT(A) function do?

_____

If you had trouble understanding what was happening to the negative values of A, don't worry at this point. We will review this completely later.

17. Jump the computer out of the input loop. Type

```
110 LET B = SGN(A)
```

Display the program and review the program structure to refresh your memory about how the program works. Execute the program for each of the following values of A. In each case, record the output.

A	Output
1.5	_____
43	_____
128.3	_____
0	_____
−1	_____

144   BASIC: A Hands-on Method

 −1.2 _____

 −345.7 _____

 4.7 _____

 −5.8 _____

Examine the output above carefully. What does the SGN function do?

_____

18. One more function. Jump the computer out of the input loop. Type

 110 LET B = ABS(A)

Execute the program for each of the values of A given below. Again, record the output in each case.

A	Output
3.4	_____
0	_____
−3.4	_____
−2	_____
2	_____
−8.45	_____
8.45	_____

Examine the output. What does the ABS function do?

_____

19. This concludes the computer work for now. Jump the computer out of the input loop and sign off.

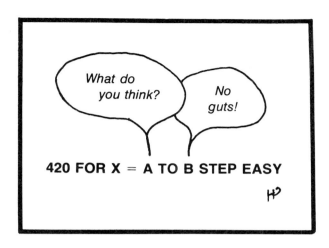

6-3 DISCUSSION

The techniques explored in the computer work can bring new power to the programs we write. We need to understand exactly how these new tools can be used to best advantage.

Built-in Looping

In the previous chapters we learned how to loop programs under the control of transfer statements. The unconditional (GO TO) statement was useful but could sometimes result in a loop with no way out. The conditional (IF THEN) statement provided a way to loop the program as desired and also a way to get out of the loop. Both of these are good techniques. However, BASIC has a very elegant way to take care of looping which takes a large burden from the back of the programmer. We will now go over this new method, which uses the FOR NEXT statements.

All FOR statements have the same format. This format and a typical statement are shown below.

Line # FOR <variable> = <relation> TO <relation> STEP <relation>
120   FOR X = 1 TO 9 STEP 2

The only things that can change or are different in FOR statements are the variable and the three relations. If the STEP is left out of the statement, the computer will use a step size of 1. We can write many different forms of the FOR statement. A few are given below to illustrate the range of possibilities.

```
130 FOR J = 2 TO 8
130 FOR T = 25 TO 10 STEP -2
130 FOR W = -20 TO 10 STEP 2
130 FOR X = 3*Z TO A*B STEP D
```

In general, we can write any legal BASIC statement in the relations involved in the FOR statement provided, of course, that the variables used have been properly defined in the program.

Use FOR NEXT statements for looping.

The FOR statement opens a loop. We close the loop with the NEXT statement. How this is done is illustrated in the following example:

```
200 FOR X = 2 TO 18 STEP 2 (Opens loop)
            .
            .
            .
         Program lines inside loop
            .
            .
            .
340 NEXT X (Closes loop)
```

Looping and Functions   147

In the NEXT statement, the variable must be the same as that in the FOR statement that opened the loop.

It is important to completely understand how these loops work. In the example above, when the program reaches line 200 the first time, X is set equal to 2. Then the computer works through the lines until line 340 is reached. This closes the loop and directs the computer back to line 200 and the next value of X, which in this case would be 4. The computer stays in the loop until the value of X either reaches or exceeds the limit of 18. Then, instead of going through the statements inside the loop, the computer jumps to the next line number following the NEXT statement used to close the loop. Let's look at an example to see the FOR NEXT statements in action once more.

```
100 LET A = 1
110 FOR X = 1 TO 6 STEP 2
120 LET A = 2*A
130 PRINT A, X
140 NEXT X
150 END
```

Since only two variables are involved in this program (A and X), we will list the line numbers in the order the computer encounters then and the corresponding values of the variables.

Line Number	A	X
100	1	
110	1	1
120	2	1
130	2	1
140	2	3
120	4	3
130	4	3
140	4	5
120	8	5
130	8	5
140	8	7 (Jumps out of loop)
150	(Program stops)	

Study the sequence of line numbers and the corresponding values of A and X until you are certain that you understand how the FOR NEXT statements control the loop.

148 BASIC: A Hands-on Method

Quite often, more complicated loop structures are required in a program. The structure can be as involved as desired provided that the loops do not cross. The example below illustrates a segment of a program with crossed loops.

```
100    FOR A = 2 TO 20
110    FOR B = 4 TO 8

       Loops cross!

240    NEXT A
250    NEXT B
```

Another example with crossed loops is

```
100    FOR I = 0  TO 20 STEP 2
110    FOR A = 10 TO 2 STEP -1
120    FOR B = 1 TO 4

       Outer loop OK; inner loops cross!

170    NEXT A
180    NEXT B
190    NEXT I
```

The following example illustrates a complicated loop structure in which the loops are organized correctly:

Don't cross your **FOR NEXT** loops!

```
 ┌──100    FOR X = 1 TO 10
 │ ┌─110   FOR Y = 2 TO 4
 │ │            .
 │ │            .
 │ │            .
 │ └─140   NEXT Y
 │              .
 │              .
 │              .
 │   ┌─170  FOR Z = 1 TO 5
 │   │           .
 │   │           .
 │   │ ┌─210 FOR K = 20 TO 10 STEP -2
 │   │ │         .
 │   │ │         .
 │   │ │         .
 │   │ └─270 NEXT K
 │   │           .
 │   │           .
 │   │           .
 │   └──310  NEXT Z
 │               .
 │               .
 │               .
 └────410   NEXT X
```

In this example we have double loops and loops within loops. Remember, though, that any combination may be used in a program provided that lines connecting the FOR statements and their corresponding NEXT statements do not cross. If they do, the computer will signal an error and stop.

Built-in Functions

One of the advantages of a modern digital computer is that sets of instructions can be preprogrammed to accomplish any desired task. Since there are many computing tasks that are routinely needed, the manufacturers have preprogrammed some of these in the form of functions. With these built-in functions in BASIC, the programmer can perform very complicated mathematical operations without difficulty. We will look at several of these functions and see exactly how they work.

Function	Action
SQR(X)	Square root of X
INT(X)	Integer part of X
SGN(X)	Sign of X
ABS(X)	Absolute value of X

Let's use the first function, SQR(X), to see how all the functions operate in general. First, X is called the argument of the function. If this definition bothers you, then think of X as "what the functions works on". If we use SQR(X) in a program, we are instructing the computer to look up the value of X, then take the square root of the number. For example,

$$SQR(36) = 6$$
$$SQR(64) = 8$$
$$SQR(100) = 10$$
$$SQR(2) = 1.41421$$

and so on. The only limitation is that we can't take the square root of a negative number. If the computer tried to evaluate SQR(-6), for example, it would signal an error and stop.

The argument of the function can be as complicated as needed in the program. If the computer runs across an expression like

$$SQR(X+4*Y)$$

it will look up the values of X and Y, carry out the calculation indicated, then take the square root. This characteristic is true for all the functions.

INT(X) takes the integer part of X. The term integer is just a high-class way to say "whole number." Thus, 2 is an integer while 23.472 is not. If we take the integer part of a number, we simply forget about everything following the decimal point. Thus

$$\begin{aligned} \text{INT}(3.1593) &= 3 \\ \text{INT}(54.76) &= 54 \\ \text{INT}(0.362) &= 0 \end{aligned}$$

However, negative numbers require special attention. What is really happening when we take the integer part of a number is that we go to the first integer less than or equal to the number. Using this rule we see that

$$\begin{aligned} \text{INT}(-2) &= -2 \\ \text{INT}(-.93) &= -1 \end{aligned}$$

and so on. Note carefully that the INT function does not round off a number. Often beginners are somewhat confused about this.

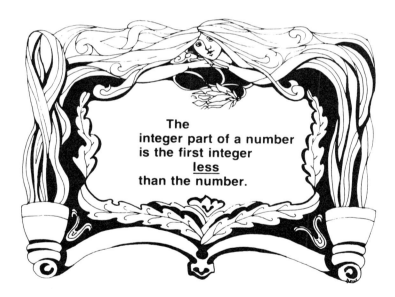

The integer part of a number is the first integer *less* than the number.

SGN(X) is a very interesting function. If X (the argument of the function) is positive, SGN(X) is +1. If X is negative, SGN(X) ia -1. If X is 0, SGN(X) is 0. In effect, SGN(X) returns the sign of X, either +1, -1, or 0. Therefore,

$$\begin{aligned} \text{SGN}(4.568) &= +1 \\ \text{SGN}(375) &= +1 \\ \text{SGN}(0) &= 0 \end{aligned}$$

SGN(−5.9031) = −1
SGN(−4) = −1

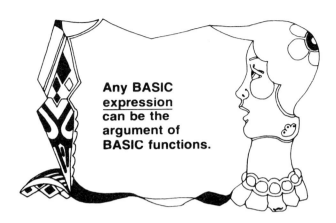

Any BASIC expression can be the argument of BASIC functions.

At this point it may not be clear to you why such a function could be useful. It turns out that the SGN function is very useful, however, and has many applications. For the time being, we will be content just to learn how the function works.

ABS(X) simply tells the computer to ignore the sign of X. In effect, it converts all values of X to positive numbers. So

ABS(4.5) = 4.5
ABS(−4.5) = 4.5
ABS(95.34) = 95.34
ABS(−95.34) = 95.34
ABS(0) = 0

There are many other built-in functions in BASIC. However, most of these involve more mathematical knowledge than we can assume in this book. If you have had the mathematics necessary to understand what the functions are doing, you will have no difficulty learning how to use them. If you are interested, consult a BASIC reference manual for your computer. We will take up some functions that involve strings of characters in Chapter 8.

The built-in functions we have been discussing are used in BASIC statements. Examples of lines that utilize such functions might be

```
100 LET X = SQR(Y)
100 LET Z = 3*INT(C)+ABS(D)
```

The built in functions can be used within functions as

100 LET Y = INT(SQR(X)+3*ABS(Z))

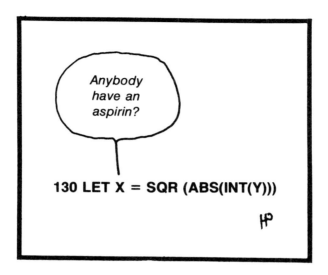

6-4 PROGRAM EXAMPLES

The example programs that we will study have been chosen to show you how we can use automatic looping and the built-in functions to make programming easier.

Example 1 — Finding the Average of a Group of Numbers

In the previous chapter, we used the problem of finding an average for one of the example programs. Let's return to the same problem but use a different method. We want the program to produce the following printout when executed:

```
HOW MANY NUMBERS (You type in)
ENTER THE NUMBERS, ONE AT A TIME
? (You type in the numbers)
THE AVERAGE IS (Computer types out average)
```

The first few lines should be easy for you to write by now.

```
100 PRINT "HOW MANY NUMBERS";
110 INPUT N
120 PRINT "ENTER THE NUMBERS, ONE AT A TIME"
```

Now we must arrange for the input of N numbers but must also keep in mind that we are supposed to compute the average of the numbers. So initially we will set S (which will be used to sum the numbers) equal to 0.

```
130 LET S = 0
```

The input of N numbers and the summing up of them is an ideal task for the FOR NEXT statements.

```
140 FOR I = 1 TO N
150 INPUT X
160 LET S = S+X
170 NEXT I
```

Notice that we don't use I, the loop variable, except to count the numbers as they are input. When all the numbers are in, the computer will jump out of the loop to the next higher line number after 170. When this happens, S will contain the sum of all the values of X that were typed in. Since we know that N is the number of numbers typed in, we can immediately compute the average.

```
180 LET A = S/N
```

The rest of the program follows without difficulty.

```
190 PRINT "THE AVERAGE IS";A
200 END
```

The complete program is

```
100 PRINT "HOW MANY NUMBERS";
110 INPUT N
120 PRINT "ENTER THE NUMBERS, ONE AT A TIME"
```

```
130 LET S = 0
140 FOR I = 1 TO N
150 INPUT X
160 LET S = S+X
170 NEXT I
180 LET A = S/N
190 PRINT "THE AVERAGE IS";A
200 END
```

Example 2 - Temperature Conversion Table

In one of the earlier programs we used the relation

$$C = 5/9*(F-32)$$

to convert from degrees Fahrenheit to degrees Celsius. Now let's generate a conversion table as follows:

Degrees F	Degrees C
0	−17.7777
5	−15
10	−12.2222
etc.	
100	37.7777

First we should print out the heading and the space before the table itself begins.

```
100 PRINT "DEGREES F","DEGREES C"
110 PRINT
```

We can use a FOR NEXT loop to generate the values of F, which can then be converted to C and printed out.

```
120 FOR F = 0 TO 100 STEP 5
130 LET C = 5*(F-32)/9
140 PRINT F,C
150 NEXT F
```

Finally we need the END statement.

```
160 END
```

The whole program is given below.

```
100 PRINT "DEGREES F","DEGREES C"
110 PRINT
120 FOR F = 0 TO 100 STEP 5
130 LET C = 5*(F-32)/9
140 PRINT F,C
150 NEXT F
160 END
```

Example 3 - Exact Division

We now want to write a program that will compute all the integers (whole numbers) that divide exactly into another integer. To illustrate, suppose we take 8 as the test integer. The problem is to find all the integers that will divide exactly into 8 with no remainder. The rule to use is

If N/X = INT(N/X) then there is no remainder

If N/X <> INT(N/X) then there is a remainder

Now let's write a program to produce the following output when executed:

```
INPUT A POSITIVE WHOLE NUMBER? (You type in)
THE NUMBERS WHICH DIVIDE EXACTLY ARE
(Computer types out first number, computer types out
second number, etc.)
```

The program begins easily.

```
100 PRINT "INPUT A POSITIVE WHOLE NUMBER";
110 INPUT N
120 PRINT "THE NUMBERS WHICH DIVIDE EXACTLY ARE"
```

Now we have to look at each of the whole numbers between 1 and N. Of course, this is ideal for the FOR NEXT loops. Using the rule given above, we can see whether or not each number divides exactly.

```
130 FOR X = 1 TO N
140 IF N/X <> INT(N/X) THEN 160
150 PRINT X,
160 NEXT X
```

Finally we need the END statement.

```
170 END
```

The complete program is

```
100 PRINT "INPUT A POSITIVE WHOLE NUMBER";
110 INPUT N
120 PRINT "THE NUMBERS WHICH DIVIDE EXACTLY ARE"
130 FOR X = 1 TO N
140 IF N/X <> INT(N/X) THEN 160
150 PRINT X,
160 NEXT X
170 END
```

You might try the program out using fairly large values of N. How could you make the program run in half the time?

Example 4 – Depreciation Schedule

When a company invests in equipment, the investment is depreciated over a number of years for tax purposes. This means that the value of the equipment is decreased each year (due to use, wear, and tear), and the amount of decrease is a tax-deductible item. One of the methods used to compute depreciaton is the "sum-of-the-digits" schedule.

To illustrate, suppose a piece of equipment has a lifetime of 5 years. The sum of the years digits would be

$$1+2+3+4+5 = 15$$

The depreciation the first year will be 5/15 of the initial value. The depreciation fraction the second year will be 4/15, and so on. If the equipment had an intial value of $3000, the depreciation schedule would be

End of Year	Depreciation Fraction	Depreciation	Current Value
1	5/15	1000	2000
2	4/15	800	1200
3	3/15	600	600
4	2/15	400	200
5	1/15	200	0

Our problem is to write a BASIC program to generate depreciation schedules by the sum-of-the-years-digits method. The output should be as follows:

```
WHAT IS THE INITIAL ASSET VALUE? (You type in)
WHAT IS THE ASSET LIFE IN YEARS? (You type in)

END OF    DEPRECIATION      DEPRECIATION      CURRENT
YEAR      FRACTION                            ASSET VALUE

          (Computer prints out table)
```

The first few lines of the program can be written without any explanation:

```
100 PRINT "WHAT IS THE INITIAL ASSET VALUE";
110 INPUT P
120 PRINT "WHAT IS THE ASSET LIFE IN YEARS";
130 INPUT N
140 PRINT
150 PRINT "END OF","DEPRECIATION","DEPRECIATION",
        "CURRENT"
160 PRINT "YEAR OF","FRACTION"," ","ASSET VALUE"
170 PRINT
```

Next we must compute the sum-of-the-years digits.

```
180 LET S = 0
190 FOR I = 1 TO N
200 LET S = S+I
210 NEXT I
```

Now we compute the schedule and print it out. We will use the variable P1 to keep track of the current asset value.

```
220 LET P1 = P
230 FOR I = 1 TO N
240 LET F = (N+1-I)/S
250 LET D = P*F
260 LET P1 = P1-D
270 PRINT I,F,D,P1
280 NEXT I
```

In line 240, F is the depreciation fraction for the Ith year. You can check this out for various values of I to ensure that the expression does generate the correct value of F. In line 250, D is the depreciation. The only thing missing now is the END statement.

```
                290 END
```

The complete program is

```
100 PRINT "WHAT IS THE INITIAL ASSET VALUE";
110 INPUT P
120 PRINT "WHAT IS THE ASSET LIFE IN YEARS";
130 INPUT N
140 PRINT
150 PRINT "END OF","DEPRECIATION","DEPRECIATION","CURRENT"
160 PRINT "YEAR","FRACTION"," ","ASSET VALUE"
170 PRINT
180 LET S = 0
190 FOR I = 1 TO N
200 LET S = S + I
210 NEXT I
220 LET P1 = P
230 FOR I = 1 TO N
240 LET F = (N+1-I)/S
250 LET D = P*F
260 LET P1 = P1-D
270 PRINT I,F,D,P1
280 NEXT I
290 END
```

Try out the program for different inputs. Of course, you can use this to set up schedules to be used on your tax returns. Impress the Internal Revenue Service with your computer-generated depreciation schedules!

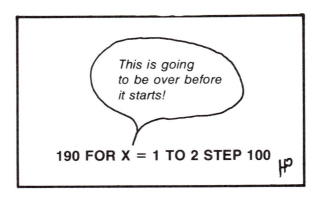

6-5 PROBLEMS

1. Write a program to generate a table of numbers and their square roots. The table should look as follows:

N	SQR(N)
2.0	1.41421
2.1	1.44914
2.2	1.48324
etc.	
3.9	1.97484
4.0	2.00000

2. Write a program to count and print out by tens going from 0 to 500.

3. Write a program to accept the input of a number N, then print out the even numbers greater than 0 but less than or equal to N.

4. Write a program to print out a conversion table from inches to centimeters. There are 2.54 centimeters in an inch. Include the appropriate headings. Start the table at 0 and continue to 10 inches in steps of 0.5 inch.

5. What will be printed out if the following program is run?

```
100 FOR X = 10 TO 1 STEP - 1
110 PRINT TAB(X);"ABCDEFGHIJ"
120 NEXT X
130 END
```

6. Trace the following program. What will be output if it is executed?

```
100 FOR I = 1 TO 5
110 READ A
120 LET B = INT(A)-SGN(A)*2
130 PRINT B
140 NEXT I
150 DATA 2.2,-3,10,0,-1.5
160 END
```

7. What will be printed out if we execute the following program?

```
100 FOR X = 1 TO 10
120 LET Y = 2*X
130 FOR Z = 1 TO 5
```

```
140 LET U = Z + Y
150 FOR V = 1 TO 3
160 PRINT V + U
170 NEXT Z
180 NEXT V
190 NEXT X
200 END
```

8. The following program won't work. What's wrong?

```
100 FOR X = -10 TO +10 STEP 2
110 PRINT X,SQR(X)
120 NEXT X
130 END
```

9. Explain what the following program does:

```
100 FOR X = 1 TO 5
110 READ Y
120 LET Z = INT(100*Y+.5)/100
130 PRINT Z
140 NEXT X
150 DATA 1.06142,27.5292,138.021
160 DATA .423715,51.9132
170 END
```

10. Write a program to print out the following pattern of asterisks.:

```
******
 *****
  ***
   *
```

No fair using more than three PRINT statements!

11. What will be printed out if the following program is executed?

```
100 LET A = 5436.12
110 FOR I = 1 TO 5
120 LET B = A/10
```

```
130 LET C = 10*(B-INT(B))
140 PRINT C
150 LET A = INT(B)
160 NEXT I
170 END
```

12. N! is read "N factorial" and means the product of all the whole numbers from 1 to N inclusive. For example

$$3! = (1)(2)(3) = 6$$
$$5! = (1)(2)(3)(4)(5) = 120$$

and so on. Write a program to call for the input of N. Then compute and print out N! If you try out this program on the computer, you may be suprised to find that values of N less than 100 produce factorials too large for the computer to handle. The factorial of N is an extremely rapidly increasing function.

13. Write a BASIC program to call for N grades to be input. Compute and print out (1) the highest grade, (2) the lowest grade, and (3) the average of the grades.

14. What, if anything, is wrong with the following program?

```
100 FOR X = 1 TO 2
110 FOR Y = 2 TO 6
120 PRINT X+Y
130 NEXT Y
140 FOR Z = 1 TO 3
150 PRINT X+Z
160 NEXT X
170 NEXT Z
180 END
```

15. What will be output if the following program is executed?

```
100 FOR X = 1 TO 4
110 FOR Y = 1 TO 3
120 LET Z = X*Y
130 PRINT Z,
140 NEXT Y
150 PRINT
160 NEXT X
170 END
```

16. Suppose you decide to invest $1000 on the first of each year for 10 years at an annual interest rate of 6 percent. At the end of the tenth year, the value of the investment will be $13,971.64. To see how this could be computed, use the following formula:

$$\$NEW = (\$OLD + I)(1 + R/100).$$

In this formula, R is the annual interest rate in percentage. I is the annual investment, $OLD is the value of the investment at the beginning of each year, and $NEW is the value of the investment at the end of the year. Thus, $NEW becomes $OLD for the next year. Write a BASIC program which will produce the following output when executed:

```
WHAT IS THE ANNUAL INVESTMENT? (You type in)
WHAT IS THE ANNUAL INTEREST RATE (%)? (You type in)
HOW MANY YEARS? (You type in)
AT THE END OF THE LAST YEAR THE
VALUE OF THE INVESTMENT WILL BE (Computer types answer)
```

17. The DATA statements below contain the time worked by a number of employees during a 1-week period.

```
190 DATA 5
200 DATA 2,4.8,8,10,8,7,10
201 DATA 5,3.75,7,8,8,6,10
202 DATA 1,3.25,8,10,6,8,8
203 DATA 4,5,8,10,6,10,6
204 DATA 3,4.25,6,6,8,10,7
```

The number in line 190 gives the number of employees to follow. Each of the DATA lines after line 190 contains a weekly record for one employee. The data are an employee number, the hourly rate, and the hours worked Monday through Friday. The employee receives time and a half for everything over 40 hours per week. Write a BASIC program using these DATA statements to compute and print out the employee number and the gross pay for the week for each of the employees.

18. Assume that the following DATA statements give the performance of the students in an English class on three examinations:

```
190 DATA 6
200 DATA 3,90,85,92
201 DATA 1,75,80,71
202 DATA 6,100,82,81
203 DATA 5,40,55,43
204 DATA 2,60,71,68
205 DATA 4,38,47,42
```

The number in line 190 is the number of student in the class. Each of the DATA statements that follow gives the performance for a single student. The information is the student ID number, grade 1, grade 2, and grade 3. Thus, as shown in line 202, student 6 got examination grades of 100, 82, and 81. Write a program using these DATA statements to computer and print out each student's ID number and his or her course grade. Assume that the first two examination grades are weighted 25 percent each toward the overall grade and the last grade is weighted 50 percent.

6-6 PRACTICE TEST

See how well you have learned the material in the chapter by taking this practice test. The answers are given at the end of the book.

1. What will be printed if the following program is executed?

```
100 FOR Y = 20 TO 1 STEP -2
110 PRINT Y,
120 NEXT Y
130 END
```

2. What will be printed out if the following program is executed?

```
100 FOR A = 1 TO 4
110 FOR B = 1 TO 3
120 PRINT A*B,
130 NEXT B
140 NEXT A
150 END
```

3. Fill in the blanks.

   a. SQR(36) =

   _____

   b. INT(7.13) =

   _____

   c. ABS(-22.8) =

   _____

   d. SGN(-1.3) =

   _____

4. What (if anything) is wrong with the following program?

```
100 FOR I = 1 TO 5
110 FOR J = 2 TO 5
120 PRINT I,J
130 NEXT I
140 NEXT J
150 END
```

5. Miles can be converted to kilometers by multiplying the number of miles by 1.609. Write a program to produce the following output when executed.

```
      Miles              Kilometers
      -----              ----------

       10                 16.09
       15                 24.135
       20                 32.18

                etc.

      100                160.9
```

6. Numerical information is loaded into DATA statements as follows:

```
100 DATA 10
110 DATA 25,21,24,21,26,27,25,24,23,24
```

The number in line 100 gives the number of numbers to be processed in the rest of the DATA statements. Write a program using these statements to compute the average of the numbers excluding the one in line 100.

7
Working with Collections of Numbers

7-1 OBJECTIVES

In this chapter we will apply some of the ideas learned earlier to collections of numbers. New concepts will be introduced which will expand the capability of BASIC. The objectives are as follows.

Single- and Double-Subscripted Variables

Much more powerful programs can be written using subscripted variables. Therefore we will see what subscripted variables are and how to use them.

Matrix Commands

BASIC has a built-in capability that enables us to handle whole collections of numbers with a single command. We need to see how these commands can be used in programs.

Program Applications

We will study BASIC programs that take advantage of the power of both subscripted variables and matrix commands.

170 BASIC: A Hands-on Method

7-2 DISCOVERY EXERCISES

Since students tend to have difficulty with this material, some introduction is needed before the computer work is started.

Subscripts

When working with groups of numbers we must be able to distinguish members of the group from one another. This is the reason for subscripts. Before getting into subscripts, however, we need to add two important words to our computer vocabulary. We could use the word collection to describe a group of numbers, but it turns out that two other words are more commonly used. The words are matrix and array. For our purposes they both mean the same thing: a "collection of numbers." If you had seen the terms matrix and array before understanding a little about what the words mean you might have gotten unnecessarily excited. Remember, then, the terms matrix and array mean a collection of numbers.

To see how this works, let's look at the array given below.

$$Y_1 = 9$$
$$Y_2 = 10$$
$$Y_3 = 7$$
$$Y_4 = 14$$
$$Y_5 = 12$$
$$Y_6 = 15$$

Working With Collections of Numbers **171**

The name of the array is Y. Its size is six, since there are six elements (or numbers) in it. The numbers 9, 10, 7, 14, 12, and 15 are the elements in the array. The numbers printed to the right and slightly below the Ys are called subscripts. Each subscript merely points to one element in the array. Thus, Y(4) means the fourth number in the array, which in this case is 14. We read Y(4) as "Y sub four." The third number in the array would be called "Y sub three," and so on. This array is one-dimensional, since it takes only a single number (or subscript) to locate a given element in the array.

Now let's look at a more complicated example but one which still uses the ideas introduced above.

$$Z_{1,1} = 4 \quad Z_{1,2} = 10 \quad Z_{1,3} = 5$$
$$Z_{2,1} = 3 \quad Z_{2,2} = 8 \quad Z_{2,3} = 7$$

In this example there are six elements in the array Z. However, this is a two-dimensional array, since we must specify which row and column we want. The first subscript gives the row number; the second specifies the column. Z(2,1) is read as "Z sub two one" and means the element of Z at the second row and first column. Likewise, the element at row 1, column 3 would be identified as Z(1,3) and would be read "Z sub one three."

To sum up, we will work with two kinds of matrices or arrays. The one-dimensional array needs only a single number to locate an element in that array. The two-dimensional array needs two numbers (a row number and a column number) to locate an element. The one-dimensional array is also associated with the idea of a single-subscripted variable. Likewise, the double-subscripted variable is used in the two-dimensional array. With this brief introduction, you are ready for the computer work.

172 BASIC: A Hands-on Method

Computer Work

1. Sign on the computer and enter the following program:

```
100 LET X(1) = 21
110 LET X(2) = 13
120 LET X(3) = 16
130 LET X(4) = 8
140 LET X(5) = 11
150 PRINT X(1)
160 END
```

What do you think will be printed out if we execute the program?

_____

Execute the program and record what happened.

_____

Working With Collections of Numbers   173

2. Now modify the program to print out the fourth value of X. Execute the program. Did it work?

_____

3. OK, type

        150 PRINT X(3) + X(4)

Display the program and study it briefly. What do you think will happen if we execute the program?

_____

Execute the program and see if you were right. Record below what actually was printed out.

_____

4. Type

       150 FOR I = 1 TO 5
       152 PRINT X(I)
       154 NEXT I

Display the program. What do you think will be printed out by this program?

_____

174 BASIC: A Hands-on Method

See if you were right. Record below what happened when you executed the program.

_____

5. Modify this program to print out only the first three values of the array X. Record below what happened when you tried this.

_____

6. Again modify the program, but this time so that the first value of the array, then every other one, will be printed out. Record what happened below.

_____

7. Clear out the program in your work space. Enter the following program:

```
100 LET Y(1,1) = 2
110 LET Y(1,2) = 5
120 LET Y(1,3) = 1
130 LET Y(2,1) = 2
140 LET Y(2,2) = 4
150 LET Y(2,3) = 3
160 PRINT Y(1,3)
170 END
```

Display the program and make sure you have entered it correctly. What do you think this program does?

_____

Execute the program and record what was printed out.

_____

Working With Collections of Numbers 175

8. Type

$$160 \text{ PRINT } Y(2,2) + Y(1,3) + Y(1,1)$$

Display the program. What will this program do if executed?

___

Execute the program and see if you were right.

___

9. Type

```
160 LET S = 0
162 FOR J = 1 TO 3
164 LET S = S+Y(1,J)
166 NEXT J
168 PRINT S
```

Display the program and study it carefully. What will happen if we execute this program?

___

Execute the program and record what was printed out.

___

176 BASIC: A Hands-on Method

Explain in your own words what is taking place in the program.

_____

10. Type

```
162 FOR I = 1 TO 2
164 LET S = S+Y(I,2)
166 NEXT I
```

Display the program. What is the program doing now?

_____

Execute the program and write down what was printed out.

_____

Again try to explain in your own words what is happening.

_____

11. Now type

```
162 FOR I = 1 TO 2
164 FOR J = 1 TO 3
166 LET S = S+Y(I,J)
168 NEXT J
170 NEXT I
172 PRINT S
180 END
```

Working With Collections of Numbers **177**

Display the program and think a minute about it. In particular, compare what you see now to what was going on in steps 9 and 10. What does this program do?

___

Execute the program and record what was typed out.

___

12. Clear out the program in your work space. Type in the following program:

```
100 DIM X(12),Y(12)
110 FOR I = 1 TO 12
120 READ X(I),Y(I)
130 NEXT I
140 PRINT X(1) + Y(4)
150 DATA 2,1
151 DATA -1,3
152 DATA 5,6
153 DATA 2,4
154 DATA 3,1
155 DATA 8,4
156 DATA 5,1
157 DATA 3,4
158 DATA 6,2
159 DATA 1,1
160 DATA 7,7
161 DATA 5,3
170 END
```

Display the program and check to see that you have entered it correctly. Study the program carefully. If we execute the program, what will be typed out?

___

178   BASIC: A Hands-on Method

Execute the program and see whether or not you were right. Record below what was typed out.

_____

13. Type

$$100$$

Now display the program. What has happened?

_____

Execute the program and record what happened.

_____

Does the DIM statement that was originally present in the program appear to be necessary?

_____

14. Type

```
100 DIM X(9),Y(9)
110 FOR I = 1 TO 9
```

Display the program. What will happen now if we execute the program?

_____

Try it and see if you were correct.

___

15. Type

    100

Doing this deleted line 100 from the program. Will the program work now that the DIM statement has been taken out?

___

Try it and record the output.

___

Compare the results of step 13 with those of step 15. Sometimes the DIM statement must be present and other times it need not be. We will return to this question later.

___

16. Clear out the program in your work space. Type in the following program:

    100 DIM A(4,3)
    110 FOR I = 1 TO 4

```
120 FOR J = 1 TO 3
130 READ A(I,J)
140 NEXT J
150 NEXT I
160 FOR I = 1 TO 4
170 FOR J = 1 TO 3
180 PRINT A(I,J);
190 NEXT J
200 PRINT
210 PRINT
220 NEXT I
230 DATA 1,3,1
240 DATA 4,2,5
250 DATA 1,4,2
260 DATA 3,2,5
270 END
```

Make sure that you have entered the program correctly, then take a few minutes to study it. Can you see what will be printed out if we execute the program?

Execute the program and record the output.

Compare what was printed out to the numbers in the DATA statements in the program.

17. Clear out the program in your work space and then enter the following program:

```
100 DIM A(4,3)
110 MAT READ A
120 MAT PRINT A;
130 DATA 1,3,1
140 DATA 4,2,5
150 DATA 1, 4, 2
160 DATA 3, 2, 5
170 END
```

Execute the program and compare the output with that obtained from the program in step 16. Do the programs accomplish the same thing?

_____

18. Type

        100 DIM A(4,3),B(4,3)
        115 MAT B = A
        120 MAT PRINT B;

Display the program. What will be output if we execute it?

_____

Now execute the program and record what was typed out.

_____

19. Clear out the program in work space. Then enter the following program:

        100 DIM X(3,3)
        110 MAT INPUT X
        120 PRINT
        130 PRINT
        140 MAT PRINT X;
        150 END

Execute the program and when the INPUT prompt comes up, type

        2,1,3,4,7,5,1,2,6

182 BASIC: A Hands-on Method

What happened?

_____

Compare the output to the numbers you typed in.

20. This concludes the computer work for this chapter. Sign off the computer.

7-3 DISCUSSION

Usually most students are a bit confused at this point about arrays and matrix commands. Therefore it is important that you pay particular attention to the discussion material to clear up any questions that might have arisen in the computer work.

Single- and Double-Subscripted Variables

The need for subscripted numbers becomes obvious when we must handle large collections of numbers. If, for example, we were writing a program that involved only four numbers, we would have no difficulty naming them. We might call the numbers X, Y, U, and V. But suppose we needed to work with 100 numbers? For this reason, it is often very useful to have subscripted numbers. Fortunately, BASIC has provisions for subscripts which are ready and waiting for our use.

Consider the following set of numbers:

i	Y_i
1	14
2	8
3	9
4	11
5	16
6	20
7	5
8	3

We can refer to the entire set of numbers with the single name Y. Thus, Y is a collection of numbers, a matrix, or an array—all of which mean roughly the same thing for our purposes. To locate a number in an array, we must have the array name (in this case Y) and the position within the array. Here is where the i column is used. Thus Y(3) (which we read as "Y sub three") locates the third number in the array Y. In this case, Y(3) has the value 9. Likewise, Y(7), is 5, Y(1) is 14, and so on. Most generally we can speak of Y(I) (which would be pronounced "Y sub I"), which denotes any element of the array depending on the value of I. If I were 8, then Y(I) would be 3 in our example. This collection of numbers is one-dimensional, since only one number (subscript) is needed to locate any element in the array.

Next let's look at a two-dimensional array.

$Y_{i,j}$	1	2	3	4
1	3	−1	10	8
2	2	4	5	6
3	1	−2	9	3

Now we need two numbers to locate an element in the array. Given a row number and a column number, we can find any element of the array we desire. For example, Y(1,3) means the element of Y located at row 1, column 3. In the example above, the element has the value 10. In general, we denote an element in the two-dimensional array as Y(I,J). The first subscript (I) is the row number, and the second subscript (J) is the column number. At this point a caution is in order. Some computers have this convention reversed and give the column number first. Check out your computer and see which subscript is given first.

To make sure you understand how the double subscripts are used, refer to the two-dimensional array in the table above and verify that the following statements are correct:

$$Y_{3,2} = -2$$
$$Y_{1,4} = 8$$
$$Y_{3,3} = 9$$
$$Y_{2,1} = 2$$

An interesting question comes up. Does X(M−N+3,S*T) mean anything? The answer is yes provided that the computer can convert M−N+3 and S*T into numbers. Even Y(Y(1,1),Y(2,3)) is all right as long as the computer can locate the numbers in Y(1,1) and Y(2,3). However, there is an important point to be remembered. Suppose we want to look up X(A+B) where A = 2.6 and B = 1.1. Thus, A+B = 3.7. But it doesn't make any sense to try to look up the 3.7th number in the array X. Accordingly, the computer will take the integer part of 3.7, and X(A+B) works out to be X(3), the third element in the array X.

Saving Space for Arrays

The computer must know how big an array is for two reasons. First, there is a question of how much space to save in memory to hold the array. Next, the computer must know the size of the array in order to carry out arithmetic operations properly. Actually, for small arrays, BASIC saves space automatically. If a one-dimensional array is used in a program, BASIC automatically sets up space for ten elements if there is no DIM statement. If a two-dimensional array is used, BASIC will save enough space in memory for a ten by ten array if no DIM statement is in the program. It probably isn't wise to use this feature of BASIC. In this book we will emphasize the routine use of dimension statements in all programs regardless of the size of the arrays.

Working With Collections of Numbers

Save space with a DIM statement.

An example of a DIM (for "dimension") statement is

```
100 DIM B(5,20),Y(8),Z(34),X(3,6)
```

Four arrays are dimensioned in line 100. B is a two-dimensional array having five rows and twenty columns. Y is one-dimensional, with eight elements. Likewise, Z is one-dimensional, with thirty-four elements. Finally, X is a two-dimensional array with three rows and six columns. It's a good practice to make the DIM statement the first one of the program. This way it is easy to glance at the beginning of the program to see the sizes of the arrays that will be used. At any rate, the DIM statement must be before any other statements that refer to arrays. As indicated above, it is also a good practice to use a DIM statement in all progams, whether or not BASIC demands it.

Subscripted Variables and FOR NEXT Loops.

Since subscripts involve collections of numbers and operations with collections of numbers almost always involve repetition, it seems reasonable that we should employ FOR NEXT statements to handle arrays. We will use FOR NEXT loops to define the subscripts used in the arrays. As an example, the following program segment will set up a six by four array, then load 5s into all the elements.

```
100 DIM A(6,4)
110 FOR R = 1 TO 6
120 FOR C = 1 TO 4
130 LET A(R,C) = 5
140 NEXT C
150 NEXT R
```

If we trace this program segment, the details of the process become clear. When line 130 in the program is reached the first time, R = 1 and C = 1. Then R is held constant while C goes to 2, 3, and 4. At each step in this process, the corresponding element of the array is set equal to 5. Then R is set equal to 2, and C takes on the values 1, 2, 3, and 4. The process goes on until all the elements of the array have been set equal to 5.

Either one- or two-dimensional arrays can be handled in this fashion using subscripts. In many applications it is preferable to use FOR NEXT loops to carry out the desired operations on arrays. However, BASIC has some special commands that can make our programming much easier.

MAT Commands in BASIC

Arrays are used so often that BASIC has special commands to handle them. These are the MAT (for "matrix") commands. We will look at only a few MAT commands since some become involved in mathematics that is past the level of this book. Specifically, we will look at the following:

```
MAT ZER
MAT INPUT
MAT READ
MAT PRINT
MAT =
```

The MAT ZER command is used to load a matrix (or array) with 0s. For example,

```
100 DIM Z(10,10)
110 MAT Z = ZER
```

defines a ten by ten matrix named Z and loads 0s into all the elements of the array. It is possible to dimension the array in the MAT statement. We could have accomplished the same thing with a single statement.

```
100 MAT Z = ZER(10,10)
```

However, as indicated above, we will stick to the practice of always using a dimension statement to specify the size of the arrays.

A useful programming trick is to save a block of space in a DIM statement, then specify within the program how much space will be used each time the program is executed. The program segment below shows how this might be done.

```
100 DIM X(100)
110 INPUT N
120 MAT X = ZER(N)
```

Here the variable N is used to dimension that portion of the 100 spaces in X that will be used. Any value of N up to and including 100 is all right. The value of N may change each time the program is executed as long as it doesn't exceed 100. In effect, this enables an array to have a variable size.

We cannot use a variable in a DIM statement on most computers. Thus

```
100 INPUT N
110 DIM X(N)
120 MAT X = ZER
```

most likely will not be accepted by your computer. However you can try and see if your computer will permit this operation.

The MAT INPUT and MAT READ statements operate the same as the INPUT and READ statements that we have been using except that collections of numbers rather than single numbers are handled. An example of the MAT READ statement in a program is given below.

```
100 DIM X(3,4)
110 MAT READ X
120 DATA 3,2,4,1
130 DATA 1,-1,0,2
140 DATA 6,3,1,8
150 END
```

The array

$$\begin{bmatrix} 3 & 2 & 4 & 1 \\ 1 & -1 & 0 & 2 \\ 6 & 3 & 1 & 8 \end{bmatrix}$$

is read from the DATA statements row by row. As organized here, one row of the array is included in each DATA statement. This is probably the nicest way to handle the DATA statements, but BASIC certainly doesn't require it. For example, we could just as well have had the following program segment:

```
100 DIM X(3,4)
110 MAT READ X
DATA 3,2,4,1,1,-1,0,2,6,3,1,8
END
```

In this program all the data are in the same DATA statement. However, it is certainly more difficult to follow what is taking place in the second program than what is happening in the first. It is strictly a matter of choice how you prefer to handle the data.

MAT INPUT acts the same way as MAT READ except that the numbers in the array must be typed in at the keyboard instead of being taken from DATA statements.

```
100 DIM Z(5,2)
110 MAT INPUT Z
```

This program segment causes the computer to type out a question mark as an INPUT prompt. The computer will then wait for ten numbers to be typed in separated by commas. The first two numbers typed in will form row 1, the second two will form row 2, and so on.

The MAT PRINT statement is best explained with an example. Suppose that the program

```
100 DIM X(2,3)
110 MAT INPUT X
120 MAT PRINT X
130 END
```

is executed, and when the INPUT prompt comes up, we type in the numbers in the matrix below, row by row.

$$\begin{bmatrix} 2 & 4 & 1 \\ 3 & 1 & 2 \end{bmatrix}$$

The output from the program will be as follows:

```
        2
        4
        1

        3
        1
        2
```

The correct numbers in the array were typed out, but the rows were typed out vertically. We are getting a carriage return after each number is printed. The problem can be cured easily by putting a semicolon after the X in the print statement.

Now with the same input, the program will print out

```
        2       4       1
        3       1       2
```

Finally, MAT = is a quick way of copying the elements of one array into another. For example

```
100 DIM X(4,5),Y(4,5)
110 MAT INPUT X
120 MAT Y = X
```

will have the following results. The computer waits for twenty elements of the array X to be typed in. Then array Y is set equal to array X term by term. It should be clear that the MAT = command can be used only if the two arrays involved have the same dimensions.

7-4 PROGRAM EXAMPLES

The use of subscripted variables as well as the MAT commands permits many interesting problems to be handled easily in BASIC. We will look at several programs to illustrate how subscripts are used and the way MAT commands save programming effort.

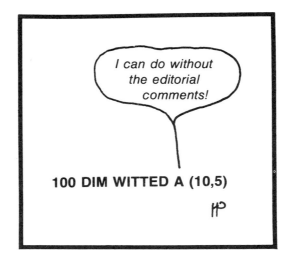

Example 1 – Examination Grades

To illustrate the concept of a one-dimensional array, let's take an example that is near and dear to the hearts of most students—a set of examination grades. Suppose that we have the following results on an examination given to a class of fifteen students:

	Student Number														
	1	2	3	4	5	6	7	8	9	10	11	12	13	14	15
Grade	67	82	94	75	48	64	89	91	74	71	65	83	72	69	72

The problem is to write a BASIC program to allow the class grades above to be typed in. The format should appear as follows:

```
HOW MANY STUDENTS?  (You type in)
        STUDENT          GRADE

           1                (You type in grade, etc.)
           2
           3

        (etc.)
```

Working With Collections of Numbers 191

The program should compute the class average, the highest grade, and the lowest grade, and print this information out as follows:

```
CLASS AVERAGE IS (Computer prints out average)
HIGHEST GRADE IS (Computer prints out highest)
LOWEST GRADE IS (Computer prints out lowest grade)
```

As in past exercises, let's take this by steps. First, since we are going to store the student grades in subscripted form, we must include a DIM statement to save space for the array.

```
100 DIM G(50)
```

We are using the variable. G to store grades and can insert up to fifty grades. Next we have a message, an input, and a space.

```
110 PRINT "HOW MANY STUDENTS";
120 INPUT N
130 PRINT
```

Now we are ready to input the grades. First the heading for the table must be generated.

```
140 PRINT "STUDENTS","GRADE"
150 PRINT
```

A loop using FOR NEXT statements is ideal to control the input of grades.

```
160 FOR I = 1 TO N
170 PRINT I,
180 INPUT G(I)
190 NEXT I
```

The student number is printed out in line 170. In line 180, the student number (I) is used as a subscript for the grade. This generates grades in the computer in the form G(1), G(2),...,G(N). The next task is to find the average of the grades. This can be done by summing up all the grades and dividing by the number of grades.

```
200 LET S = 0
210 FOR I = 1 TO N
220 LET S = S+G(I)
230 NEXT I
240 PRINT
```

Now we compute the average and print out the results.

```
250 LET M = S/N
260 PRINT "CLASS AVERAGE IS";M
```

The final part of the program is to locate and print out the highest and lowest grades in the class. H and L will stand for the highest and lowest grades, respectively. Initially we will set both H and L equal to G(1), the first grade in the list. We know that the same grade can't be the highest and lowest at the same time. Thus, we will go through the rest of the grades, compare H and L with each grade, and make adjustments to H and L as required.

```
270 LET H = G(1)
280 LET L = G(1)
290 FOR I = 2 TO N
300 IF L <G (I) THEN 320
310 LET L = G(I)
320 IF H >G (I) THEN 340
330 LET H = G(I)
340 NEXT I
```

The required printout can be obtained with two lines.

```
350 PRINT "HIGHEST GRADE IS";H
360 PRINT "LOWEST GRADE IS";L
```

Finally the END statement completes the program.

```
370 END
```

The complete program follows:

```
100 DIM G(50)
110 PRINT "HOW MANY STUDENTS";
120 INPUT N
130 PRINT
140 PRINT "STUDENT","GRADE"
150 PRINT
160 FOR I = 1 TO N
170 PRINT I,
180 INPUT G(I)
190 NEXT I
200 LET S = 0
210 FOR I = 1 TO N
220 LET S = S+G(I)
230 NEXT I
240 PRINT
250 LET M = S/N
260 PRINT "CLASS AVERAGE IS";M
270 LET H = G(1)
280 LET L =   G(1)
290 FOR I = 2 TO N
300 IF L < G(I) THEN 320
310 LET L = G(I)
320 IF H > G(I) THEN 340
330 LET H = G(I)
340 NEXT I
350 PRINT "HIGHEST GRADE IS";H
360 PRINT "LOWEST GRADE IS";L
370 END
```

You should sign on the computer and execute this program using the data at the beginning of the discussion. If you have any difficulty with the highest and lowest search in lines 270 through 340, trace the program in detail.

Example 2 - Course Grades

We can easily extend the ideas in Example 1 to a two-dimensional array. Now, suppose we have a class with ten students, and the course grade is based upon five examinations. Typical results for such a class might be

Student Number

		1	2	3	4	5	6	7	8	9	10
	1	92	71	81	52	75	97	100	63	41	75
	2	85	63	79	49	71	91	93	58	52	71
Exam	3	89	74	80	61	79	88	97	55	51	73
	4	96	68	84	58	80	93	95	61	47	70
	5	82	72	82	63	73	92	93	68	56	74

We will use the MAT commands to READ the data from DATA statements. The computer is to compute and print out the following information:

STUDENT	COURSE AVE
1	(Computer prints average, etc.)
2	
3	
(etc.)	

TEST	CLASS AVE
1	(Computer prints average, etc.)
2	
3	
(etc.)	

The program must start with a DIM statement although the DATA statements can go anywhere in the program.

```
100 DIM G(5,10)
```

This reserves memory space for an array with five rows and ten columns. The row number (R) will be the examination number, and the column number (C) will correspond to the student number.

```
110 DATA 92,71,81,52,75,97,100,63,41,75
120 DATA 85,63,79,49,71,91,93,58,52,71
130 DATA 89,74,80,61,79,88,97,55,51,73
140 DATA 96,68,84,58,80,93,95,61,47,70
150 DATA 82,72,82,63,73,92,93,68,56,74
```

Since the array G has already been dimensioned, all the numbers can be read into the program with a single command.

```
160 MAT READ G
```

This causes the numbers to be read into the matrix G by rows. Thus, the data in line 110 becomes row 1 of the matrix G, and so forth. Before doing anything else, we must print out the required headings.

```
170 PRINT "STUDENT","COURSE AVE"
180 PRINT
```

Now we can compute the course average for each student.

```
190 FOR C = 1 TO 10
```

Line 190 opens a loop that will look at each column in the matrix. For each value of C, we must compute the column average and print it out.

```
200 LET S = 0
210 FOR R = 1 TO 5
220 LET S = S+G(R,C)
230 NEXT R
240 PRINT C,S/5
```

Then close the C loop.

```
250 NEXT C
```

Now the process is repeated except that the averages are computed on rows rather than columns.

196 BASIC: A Hands-on Method

```
260 PRINT
270 PRINT "TEST","CLASS AVE"
280 PRINT
290 FOR R = 1 TO 5
300 LET S = 0
310 FOR C = 1 TO 10
320 LET S = S+G(R,C)
330 NEXT C
340 PRINT R,S/10
350 NEXT R
```

Finally the END statement,

```
360 END
```

The complete program follows:

```
100 DIM G(5,10)
110 DATA 92,71,81,52,75,97,100,63,41,75
120 DATA 85,63,79,49,71,91,93,58,52,71
130 DATA 89,74,80,61,79,88,97,55,51,73
140 DATA 96,68,84,58,80,93,95,61,47,70
150 DATA 82,72,82,63,73,92,93,68,56,74
160 MAT READ G
170 PRINT "STUDENT","COURSE AVE"
180 PRINT
190 FOR C = 1 TO 10
200 LET S = 0
210 FOR R = 1 TO 5
220 LET S = S+G(R,C)
230 NEXT R
240 PRINT C,S/5
250 NEXT C
260 PRINT
270 PRINT "TEST","CLASS AVE"
280 PRINT
290 FOR R = 1 TO 5
300 LET S = 0
310 FOR C = 1 TO 10
320 LET S = S + G(R,C)
330 NEXT C
340 PRINT R,S/10
350 NEXT R
360 END
```

Working With Collections of Numbers **197**

This program is an interesting one and illlustrates valuable programming techniques involving arrays. It is worth studying and executing on your computer.

Example 3 - Array Operations

The final example will consist of a series of short programs that will be given without explanation. Study each program until you are sure you understand what is taking place.

a. Write a program using FOR NEXT loops to load a three by four array with 1s.

```
100 DIM X(3,4)
110 FOR R = 1 TO 3
120 FOR C = 1 TO 4
130 LET X(R,C) = 1
140 NEXT C
150 NEXT R
160 END
```

b. Write a program using a MAT READ statement to read all 9s into a three by two array.

```
100 DIM Y(3,2)
110 MAT READ Y
120 DATA 9,9
130 DATA 9,9
140 DATA 9,9
150 END
```

c. Write a program to generate and load the numbers

2, 4, 8, 16, 32, 64, 128, 256, 512, 1024, 2048

into a one-dimensional array.

```
100 DIM Z(11)
110 LET Z(1) = 2
120 FOR I = 2 TO 11
130 LET Z(I) = 2*Z(I-1)
140 NEXT I
150 END
```

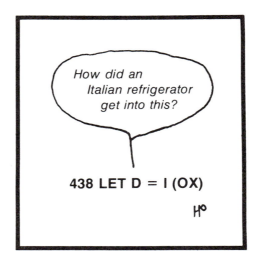

d. Write a program to read in the array

$$\begin{bmatrix} 2 & 3 & 5 \\ 1 & 4 & 2 \end{bmatrix}$$

from DATA statements and then print out the array.

```
100 DIM A(2,3)
110 MAT READ A
120 MAT PRINT A;
130 DATA 2,3,5
140 DATA 1,4,2
150 END
```

7-5 PROBLEMS

1. Without using a MAT command, write a program using the DATA statements

```
200 DATA 12
210 DATA 2,1,4,3,2,4,5,6,3,5,4,1
```

Which will read the size of an array from the first DATA statement, then read the elements of the array from the second DATA statement, loading them into an array X. Then print out the array.

Working With Collections of Numbers **199**

2. Write a program to fill a 3 by 4 array with ones.

3. Write a program to call for the input of a square N by N matrix where N is a whole number no larger than 10. Compute and print out the sum of the entries on the main diagonal of the array.

4. Write a BASIC program using a MAT READ command to read twenty-five numbers from the DATA statements into a one-dimensional array named A. Search the array and print out the number of elements in the array that are greater than fifty. Fill in the requred DATA statements with any numbers you choose.

5. Write a program to call for the input of a M by N matrix. Assume that both M and N are no larger than 15. Then compute and print out the sum of all the elements in the matrix.

6. The program below is supposed to compute and print out the sum of the elements in a one-dimensional array that are positive but not greater than 10. As it stands the program is incorrect. What's wrong?

```
100 DIM A(6)
110 MAT INPUT A
120 LET S = 0
130 FOR I = 6 TO 1 STEP -1
140 IF A(I) > 10 THEN 160
150 LET S = S+A(I)
160 NEXT I
170 PRINT S
180 END
```

7. What will be output if the following program is executed?

```
100 DIM Y(6)
110 MAT READ Y
120 DATA 2,1,3,1,2,1
130 LET S1 = 0
140 LET S2 = 0
150 FOR I = 1 TO 6
160 LET S1 = S1 + Y(I)
170 LET S2 = S2 + Y(I)^2
180 NEXT I
200 LET X = S2 - S1
210 PRINT X
220 END
```

8. What will be output if the following program is executed?

```
100 DIM A(10)
110 MAT READ A
120 LET X = A(1)
130 FOR I = 1 TO 9
140 LET A(I) = A(I+1)
150 NEXT I
160 LET A(10) = X
170 MAT PRINT A
180 DATA 10,9,8,7,6,5,4,3,2,1
190 END
```

9. What will be printed out if the following program is executed?

```
100 DIM X(4,4)
110 MAT READ X
120 DATA 1,2,3,4,2,3,4,5
130 DATA 3,4,5,6,4,5,6,7
140 LET S = 0
150 FOR I = 1 TO 4
160 LET S = S+X(I,5-I)
170 NEXT I
180 PRINT S
190 END
```

10. What will be printed out if the following program is executed?

```
100 DIM Y(4,4)
110 MAT Y = ZER
120 FOR R = 1 TO 4
130 FOR C = 1 TO 4
140 LET Y(R,C) = R*C
150 NEXT C
160 NEXT R
180 MAT PRINT Y;
190 END
```

11. Write a BASIC program to call for the input of N (assumed to be a whole number between 1 and 100), then input a one-dimensional array with N elements. Sort the array into descending order, and finally print out the sorted array.

12. Let's assume that the first number in the DATA statements gives the number of pieces of data to follow. Assume that the pieces of data are all whole numbers between 1 and 10 inclusive. Write a program that will compute the number of 1s and 2s etc., in the data and then print this out. (Hint: use the data as they are read in as a subscript to increment an element of an array used to count the numbers.)

13. What will be printed out if the following program is executed?

```
100 DIM Z(6,6)
110 MAT Z = ZER
120 FOR R = 1 TO 5 STEP 2
130 FOR C = R TO 6
140 LET Z(R,C) = 1
150 NEXT C
160 NEXT R
170 MAT PRINT Z;
180 END
```

14. If the program below is executed, what will the computer print out?

```
100 DIM A(5,5)
110 MAT READ A
120 DATA 2,2,2,2,2,2,2,2,2,2
130 DATA 2,2,2,2,2,2,2,2,2,2
140 DATA 2,2,2,2,2
150 FOR C = 5 TO 1 STEP -1
160 FOR R = 1 TO C
170 LET A(R,C) = 3
180 NEXT R
190 NEXT C
200 MAT PRINT A;
210 END
```

15. Write a program to read the following array from DATA statements, then print out the array.

$$\begin{bmatrix} 2 & 1 & 0 & 5 & 1 \\ 3 & 2 & 1 & 3 & 1 \end{bmatrix}$$

16. Write a program (not using MAT statements) to read the following array from DATA statements, then print out the array.

$$\begin{bmatrix} 5 & 3 \\ 2 & 0 \\ -1 & 1 \\ 4 & 2 \\ 2 & 6 \end{bmatrix}$$

17. Write a BASIC program that will call for the input of an M by N array. Then compute and print out the sum of the elements in each row and the product of the elements in each column.

18. Write a BASIC program that will read two arrays from DATA statements. Both the arrays are two by three. Then compute a third two by three array such that each element is the sum of the corresponding elements in the first two arrays. Print out the third array.

19. The data below represent sales totals made by salespersons over a one-week period.

		Mon	Tue	Wed	Thu	Fri	Sat
	1	48	40	73	120	100	90
	2	75	130	90	140	110	85
Salesperson	3	50	72	140	125	106	92
	4	108	75	92	152	91	87

Write a program that will compute and print out

a. The daily sales totals

b. The weekly sales totals for each salesperson

c. The total weekly sales

20. Write a program to call for the input of a 4 by 4 matrix. Compute a new matrix from the first with the rows and columns interchanged. That is, row 1 of the input matrix becomes column 1 of the new matrix. Row 2 of the input matrix becomes column 2 of the new matrix, and so on. Print out the new matrix.

21. Consider the two arrays below:

P	X
1	28
5	2
3	14
6	3
4	17
2	9

Each element of P "points" to an element of X. P(1) = 1 and X(1) = 28. P(2) = 5 and X(5) = 17. If you keep this process up, the values of X are listed in descending order. Write a program to set up two arrays X and P to some convenient length. Then call for the input of arbitrary values of X which you can type in at the keyboard. Construct the array P so that its elements point to X in descending order as illustrated above. Then print out the two arrays as shown.

7-6 PRACTICE TEST

Check yourself with the following practice test. The answers are given at the end of the book.

1. What is the purpose of the DIM statement?

2. We have an array named X. What variable name does BASIC use to locate the element in row 3, column 4?

3. Replace the program segment below with one that uses MAT statements.

```
100 FOR I = 1 TO 8
110 READ A(I)
120 NEXT I
```

4. Use a MAT INPUT statement in a progam to input a list of numbers, then find and print out the sum of the positive numbers in the list. The printout should look as follows:

```
HOW MANY NUMBERS? (You type in the number)
WHAT ARE THE NUMBERS? (You type them in)
THE SUM OF POSITIVE ELEMENTS IS (Computer types out answer)
```

5. What is the MAT ZER statement used for?

_____

6. Write a program using FOR NEXT statements to load a four by six array with 4s.

_____

7. What will be printed out if the following program is executed?

```
100 DIM A(5,5)
110 MAT A = ZER
120 FOR I = 1 TO 5
130 LET A(I, I) = 2
140 NEXT I
150 MAT PRINT A;
160 END
```

_____

8. The following array is named A:

$$\begin{bmatrix} 1 & 3 & 5 \\ 6 & 2 & 4 \end{bmatrix}$$

a. Write a DIM statement for A.

b. What is the value of A(2,3)?

c. If X = 1 and Y = 2, what is A(X,Y)?

d. What is A(A(1,1),A(2,2))?

String Variables

8-1 OBJECTIVES

Some of the most important applications of computers are non-numeric and deal with characters rather than numbers. Strings of characters can be handled as "string variables" and are the subject of this chapter. Specifically we will look at the following string-related topics.

String Input and Output

Before meaningful operations can be carried out on strings we must learn how input and output of string variables are handled on the computer.

String Functions

You have already studied BASIC functions that operated on numbers. Now we will turn to functions which work on strings of characters.

String Operations

The final goal is to write programs which work with string variables.

8-2 DISCOVERY EXERCISES

Strings are handled in somewhat different ways on various computers. From time to time you will need to refer to Appendix A to learn how to carry out specific operations on your computer. Recall that thus far in the book, all the programs had only upper-case letters. In this chapter we will depart from this practice and use "substitution" functions in lower case letters. The lower case letters will describe some process or function involving strings that must be replaced by the appropriate upper-case description needed for your computer. Remember, then, that if you see lower-case letters in a program, you must substitute the upper-case functions used on your computer.

Computer Work

1. Sign on the computer and enter the following program:

```
100 DIM A$(72)
110 INPUT A$
120 PRINT
130 PRINT A$
140 PRINT A$
150 END
```

The A$ in the program identifies the variable as a string variable. Note that the variable is dimensioned to a size of 72 which refers to the number of characters in the variable. We will return to the question of dimensioning of string variables later. Execute the program and at the input prompt (the question mark) type in your full name. What happened?

_____

2. Now modify the program as follows:

```
100 DIM A$(72),B$(72)
110 INPUT A$
115 INPUT B$
120 PRINT
130 PRINT B$
140 PRINT A$
150 END
```

If you execute the program and at the input prompt type the words INTELLIGENT and CONVERSATION separated by a comma what do you think will be printed back?

_____

Try it and record what did happen.

_____

3. Now delete line 100 from the program and execute it once more. What happened?

___

Does your computer require the DIM statement?

___

4. Let's try a different variation. Clear out the program and enter the following:

```
100 DIM X$(20),Y$(20)
110 READ X,X$,Y,Y$
120 DATA 10,"HERB",20,"CHARLIE"
130 PRINT X,Y
140 PRINT X$,Y$
150 END
```

This program contains several new ideas. What do you think will happen if you execute the program?

___

OK, execute the program and record what took place.

___

5. Now that you have seen that strings can be included in DATA statements, we should go a bit further. Change line 110 to read

110 READ X$,X,Y,Y$

210 BASIC: A Hands-on Method

What will happen if you try to execute the program in this form?

_____

See if you were right. Record below what took place when you tried to execute the program.

_____

6. Clearly, you must be careful to ensure that the type of information in the DATA statements matches the type of variable in READ statements. Now on to a different topic. Clear out the program and enter the following:

```
100 DIM C$(72)
110 INPUT C$
120 LET N = LEN(C$)
130 PRINT N
140 END
```

The new feature in this program is the function LEN(C$). It is new because it works on a string (in this case the string is C$) rather than a number. Can you guess what the function does?

_____

Notice that the result of the function LEN operating on a string must be a number since the result is assigned to a numeric variable N. Execute the program and at the input prompt type in ABCDE. What was printed back?

_____

Try it again, but this time type in AARDVARK. What happened?

_____

By now you should have a pretty good idea what the LEN function does.

8. Here's a new problem for you. If you execute the program and at the input prompt merely press the RETURN key what do you think will be printed back by the computer?

_____

Try it out and see if you were correct. Now just one more variation. Execute the program and at the input prompt type in R O B E R T. Note the spaces between the characters. What was typed back?

_____

In the LEN function, do spaces count as characters?

_____

9. Clear out the program from the work space and enter the one below:

```
100 DIM A$(72)
110 INPUT A$
120 INPUT I
130 PRINT A$(I)
140 PRINT
150 GOTO 120
160 END
```

Execute the program and at the first input prompt type in ABCDEFGHIJKLM-NOPQRSTUVWXYZ. At the second input prompt type in 20. What happened?

_____

212 BASIC: A Hands-on Method

The computer is at the input prompt for I. This time, type in 10. What happened?

_____

Experiment with various values of I between 1 and 26. Describe in your own words what happens when the computer is directed to print out A$(I).

_____

10. There is an important idea to be uncovered about your computer. You should still be at the input prompt for I. If not, execute the program again, enter the characters A through Z. Now at the input prompt for I, type in 0. What happened?

_____

The point of this is that the first character in a string is numbered zero on some computers and 1 on others. If you got an error message above you can be reasonably sure that your computer starts numbering characters in a string with the numeral 1. If you got the entire string printed back, your computer starts numbering with zero. Which ever way it works on your computer, remember it for future use.

11. There is one last thing to check. You should still be at the input prompt for I. Type in 30. What happened?

_____

By now you should understand fairly clearly what happens when the computer prints out A$(I). Of course in this instance the value of I is greater than the length of the string. We will return to this topic in the discussion section. Jump your computer out of the input loop.

12. So far we haven't had to worry about individual differences between computers. Now we come to a topic which is handled in various ways. We want to be able to specify a substring for a given string. That is, given a string A$ how can we specify the Mth through the Nth character in that string? Look up how this is done in Appendix A and record below.

> THE FUNCTION TO SET OFF THE MTH THROUGH NTH
>
> CHARACTERS IN A STRING IS _____

13. Now clear out the program in your work space and enter the one below:

```
100 DIM A$(72)
110 INPUT A$
120 PRINT "M = ";
130 INPUT M
140 PRINT "N = ";
150 INPUT N
160 PRINT seg(A$,M,N)
170 END
```

Line 160 contains the first of the substitution functions that were mentioned at the beginning of the chapter. Instead of seg(A$,M,N) you should substitute the function you copied down in step 12. Let's try it out. Execute the program at the input prompt for the string type MISSISSIPPI. Note that the length of this string is 11. Enter 4 for M and 8 for N. What happened?

_____

You should have seen the substring SISSI typed out.

14. Experiment on your own with this program. Try various strings and different values of M and N until you understand exactly how the segment function works. Remember that in the programs to follow you will not use seg(A$,M,N) but will instead substitute the appropriate function for your computer.

15. Now on to a different topic. Clear out the program in work space and enter the following:

```
100 DIM A$(72),B$(72)
110 INPUT A$
120 INPUT B$
130 IF A$ < B$ THEN 160
140 PRINT B$
150 GOTO 110
160 PRINT A$
170 GOTO 110
180 END
```

Take a few moments to study the program. Clearly, the interesting part is in line 130 where the strings A$ and B$ are involved in an IF THEN statement. In particular, what do you suppose A$ < B$ means with regard to strings?

_____

The way to find out if you are right or not is to execute the program and run a few test cases through the computer. Execute the program and at the first input prompt, type in DUCK; at the second prompt, type in CHICKEN. What was typed out?

_____

16. The computer is at the input prompt waiting for a string to be typed in. This time type in HOUSE followed by TELEVISION. What was typed out?

_____

Keep experimenting with words or letters of your choice until you see exactly what the expression A$ < B$ means. Once you understand this it should be easy for you to see what A$ = B$, A$ > B$, or A$ <> B$ would mean.

17. Jump the computer out of the input loop. Clear out the program and let's go on to the next string topic. Some of the older computers do not have these two

functions. When you check in Appendix A if your computer is not included, go on to the discussion material and skip the balance of this section. Using Appendix A, look up how to convert from a position number in the standard ASCII character set to the corresponding character. Record the function below.

> THE FUNCTION TO CONVERT A POSITION NUMBER IN
>
> THE ASCII CHARACTER SET TO THE CORRESPONDING
>
> CHARACTER IS _____

18. Enter the following program:

```
100 INPUT N
110 PRINT chr$(N)
120 GOTO 100
130 END
```

Instead of chr$(N) in line 110, substitute the function you wrote down in step 17. Now execute the program and at the input prompt, type in 65. What happened?

_____

The program will keep looping through as long as we desire. This time try 66. What happened?

_____

19. By now, the cat should be out of the bag! Play with this program trying out various numerical inputs. Keep the numbers in the range 35 to 172. Very quickly, you should see that you can refer to a character either by the character itself or by a position number in the set of characters. In the discussion section we will go over the complete character set in detail and clear up any fuzzy areas that may remain.

20. Now on to a different topic. First, clear out the program in work space. Using Appendix A, look up how to convert from a character to its equivalent position number in the standard character set. Record this below.

> THE FUNCTION TO CONVERT A CHARACTER TO THE EQUIVALENT POSITION NUMBER IN THE ASCII CHARACTER SET IS _____

Now enter the following program:

```
100 DIM A$(72)
110 INPUT A$
120 LET X = asc(A$)
130 PRINT X
140 GOTO 110
150 END
```

Instead of asc(A$) in line 120, you should substitute the function you just looked up in Appendix A. Execute the program and at the input prompt, type Z. What happened?

_____

This new function is just the reverse of chr$(N). Use various letters and numbers and try to relate what happens to your experiences in step 19.

21. There is one more detail to be seen to. Your computer should still be at the input prompt waiting for A$ to be typed in. This time type in POTATO. Note what was typed back. Then try PEA. What happened?

_____

The only similarity between the two words is that they both have the same first letter. We will return to this concept later.

22. This concludes the computer work for this chapter. Sign off the computer and go on to the next section.

8-3 DISCUSSION

Now let's go back over the ideas introduced in the computer work. This will be somewhat different than the earlier chapters since we have the notion of "substitution functions" present for the first time. Remember that when you see lower-case letters in a program, you must substitute the appropriate upper-case letters for your computer. The reason for this is that strings are handled on different computers in various ways.

String Input and Output

As you have already seen, a set of characters set off on either end by quotation marks is called a string. The quotation marks are not part of the string however. The new idea in this chapter is that the string can be treated as a variable—the string variable. The full discussion of strings was delayed until this chapter becuase of the need to dimension strings with the DIM statement that was introduced in Chapter 7.

The requirement for a DIM statement to set the maximum size of strings depends on the computer you are using. We will make it a practice to dimension all strings to some maximum length whether or not your computer requires it. If your computer does not permit strings to be dimensioned, simply delete the DIM statement from the discussion and programs that will follow.

A sample DIM statement might be

```
100 DIM A$(25),B$(72),C$(5)
```

First, the string variable is identified by appending a dollar sign ($) to a letter. Thus, the string variables in the dimension statement above are A$, B$, and C$. The numbers in the dimension statement refer to the maximum length of the string. For example, if we tried to assign the string CALIFORNIA to C$ we would get an error message back since there are 10 characters in the string and the string has been dimensioned to a maximum length of 5. We do not have to match the string with the exact dimension in the DIM statement. For example, it is perfectly all right to assign AUTO to A$ if A$ has been dimensioned to a length of 25 as in the DIM statement above. Shorter strings can be assigned as long as the length does not exceed the dimension in the DIM statement.

Input and output of string variables is handled the same way as for numeric variables. We can mix numeric and string variables in the same BASIC statements. Examples might be

```
100 PRINT A$,X,Y,Z$
110 INPUT M$,N
120 READ A$,B$,Z
```

You must be careful that the input in either INPUT or READ statements matches the type of variable given. In line 110 above, the computer would be looking for a string of characters and a number. However, you must be aware that you can type in 123456789 and if the compter is looking for a string it will identify this quantity as a string, not as a number. The reason is that the string, as has been pointed out, consists of characters. The characters 0 through 9 are part of the standard character set that will be discussed later. If, on the other hand, the computer is looking for a number and you type in ABCDEFGHI, you will get an error.

String Functions

The LEN function is used to determine the length of a string. If, for example, A$ = "HOW NOW BROWN COW" then LEN(A$) = 17. Note that the spaces are counted as characters. You can also have a "null" string. If A$ = "" (there is nothing inside the quotation marks) then LEN(A$) = 0.

A substring is a piece or segment of a string. There are several ways to deal with substrings. Consider the following program:

```
100 DIM A$(72)
110 LET A$ = "ROBERT E. LEE"
120 PRINT A$(8)
130 END
```

LEN (A$) produces the length of A$ in characters

The expression A$(8) identifies the substring of A$ consisting of the eighth character through the end of the string. If the program were run, the characters E. LEE would be printed out.

There is an important issue that you must settle. This concerns the question of what is the number of the first character in a string. On some computers the first character is numbered 0 and on others it is numbered 1. If the first character is numbered 1, then

```
120 PRINT A$(1)
```

in the example above would cause the entire string to be printed out. If the first character is numbered 0 then the result would be the string OBERT E. LEE. You should experiment with your computer and settle the issue. In this book we will assume that the first character is numbered 1. If this is not true on your computer, you should make the trivial adjustment in the programs that will be discussed.

Another way to identify a substring is with the seg function. This is illustrated in the following program:

```
100 DIM X(72)
110 LET X$ = "SUPERSONIC"
120 PRINT seg(X$,3,8)
130 END
```

Function seg(X$,3,8) identifies that part of the string X$ beginning with character number 3 and extending through character number 8. You must substitute the correct replacement function for your computer. Numeric variables can be used in the seg function as in seg(A$,M,N) which identifies the Mth through Nth characters in the string A$.

String variables can be compared in IF THEN statements. The comparison is done by alphabetical ordering. Thus A < B since A comes before B in the alphabet. CAT < DOG, HOUSE > CAR, PEA < PEARL, and so on.

The final topic that we will discuss concerns the ASCII (short for American Standard Code for Information Interchange) standard character set. This set is used on most computers and consists of one-hundred and twenty-eight characters numbered 0 through 127. The ASCII set is shown in Table 1.

Characters 0 through 31 are special purpose and have no relevancy to our discussion. The upper-case letters A through Z are numbered 65 through 90. The lower-case letters a through z are numbered 97 through 122. The numerals 0 through 9 are numbered 48 through 57. The other numbered characters include punctuation marks, arithmetic operators (+, -, *, etc.) and other special characters.

Two string functions work with the ASCII character set. First, chr$(N) returns the Nth character from the ASCII character set, For example, chr$(65) = "A", chr$(122) = "z", and so forth. We can also turn things around and convert from a character to its ASCII number. This is done with the asc(A$) function. For example, asc(A) = 65 and asc(z) = 122.

Suppose that A$ = "AIRPLANE". What is asc(A$)? Since the length of the string is greater than one, only the first character is considered. In this case the first character is A and asc(A$) = 65.

Remember that both chr$(N) and asc(A$) are substitution functions and you must replace them in programs with the functions used on your computer. These replacements can be looked up in Appendix A.

8-4 PROGRAM EXAMPLES

Several example programs should help you pull together the various concepts about strings that have been introduced in this chapter.

Example 1 - String Reversal

The task is to write a program to call for the input of a string and then print it back in reverse order. First, we must arrange for the string input.

```
100 DIM A$(72)
110 INPUT A$
```

CHR$(N)	N	CHR$(N)	N	CHR$(N)	N	CHR$(N)	N
NULL (↑@)	0	SP	32	@	64		96
SOH (↑A)	1	!	33	A	65	a	97
STX (↑B)	2	"	34	B	66	b	98
ETX (↑C)	3	#	35	C	67	c	99
EOT (↑D)	4	$	36	D	68	d	100
ENQ (↑E)	5	%	37	E	69	e	101
ACK (↑F)	6	&	38	F	70	f	102
BELL (↑G)	7	'	39	G	71	g	103
BS (↑H)	8	(	40	H	72	h	104
HT (↑I)	9	)	41	I	73	i	105
LF (↑J)	10	*	42	J	74	j	106
VT (↑K)	11	+	43	K	75	k	107
FF (↑L)	12	,	44	L	76	l	108
CR (↑M)	13	—	45	M	77	m	109
SO (↑N)	14	.	46	N	78	n	110
SI (↑O)	15	/	47	O	79	o	111
DLE (↑P)	16	0	48	P	80	p	112
DC1 (↑Q)	17	1	49	Q	81	q	113
DC2 (↑R)	18	2	50	R	82	r	114
DC3 (↑S)	19	3	51	S	83	s	115
DC4 (↑T)	20	4	52	T	84	t	116
NAK (↑U)	21	5	53	U	85	u	117
SYN (↑V)	22	6	54	V	86	v	118
ETB (↑W)	23	7	55	W	87	w	119
CAN (↑X)	24	8	56	X	88	x	120
EM (↑Y)	25	9	57	Y	89	y	121
SUB (↑Z)	26	:	58	Z	90	z	122
ESC (↑[)	27	;	59	[	91	{	123
FS (↑\)	28	<	60	\	92			124
GS (↑])	29	=	61	]	93	}	125
RS (↑^)	30	>	62	^	94	~	126
US (↑_)	31	?	63	—	95	DEL	127

Table 1 — ASCII Character Set

The next few lines print the string back in reverse order.

```
120 FOR X = LEN(A$) TO 1 STEP -1
130 PRINT seg(A$,X,X);
140 NEXT X
```

The loop steps backwards from the length of the string to 1. Of course, if your computer begins numbering the characters in a string at zero, the loop should step back to zero. The replacement function seg(A$,X,X) identifies the substring in A$ beginning with character number X and extending through character number X. This isolates a single character.

With an END statement added the complete program is

```
100 DIM A$(72)
110 INPUT A$
120 FOR X = LEN(A$) TO 1 STEP -1
130 PRINT seg(A$,X,X);
140 NEXT X
150 END
```

Replace seg(A$,X,X) with the function needed on your computer. Try out the program and see that it works as advertised.

Example 2 - Word Count

The number of words in a sentence can be determined from the number of spaces (assuming that the only purpose of a space is to separate words). The following program prints out the number of words in the input string.

```
100 DIM A$(72)
120 INPUT A$
130 LET S = 0
140 FOR I = 1 TO LEN(A$)
150 IF seg(A$,I,I) <> " " THEN 170
160 LET S = S+1
170 NEXT I
180 PRINT "WORD COUNT = ",S+1
190 END
```

Study the program until you see exactly how it works. If your computer starts the character count in a string with zero, line 140 should read

```
140 FOR I = 0 TO LEN(A$)
```

Try out the program by typing in a sentence. Verify that it works correctly.

Example 3 - Replacement Code

Suppose we want a program to encode a sentence. A simple-minded way to construct a code (which incidentally could be broken very rapidly with computers) is to replace each character in the message with another. This is done most easily by reference to the ASCII character set. However, let's do this one "from scratch".

The first part of the program calls for the input of the string to be coded and sets up the conversion scheme.

```
100 DIM A$(72),B$(29),C$(29)
110 LET B$ = "ABCDEFGHIJKLMNOPQRSTUVWXYZ ,."
120 LET C$ = "ETAVZBHCW KPSYDF,GXIMJLONQU.R"
130 INPUT A$
```

B$ contains the characters that can be used in the input string which is to be coded. C$ is the replacement key. An A in the input string is to be replaced by an E, F is replaced by B, J by a space, and so on.

Now we can examine each character and do the replacement.

```
140 FOR I = 1 TO LEN(A$)
150 FOR J = 1 TO 29
160 IF seg(A$,I,I)<> seg(B$,J,J) THEN 190
170 PRINT seg(C$,J,J);
180 GOTO 200
190 NEXT J
200 NEXT I
```

The outer I loop steps through each character in A$. The inner J loop compares the Ith character of A$ to the character in B$ until a match is found at the Jth character. When this happens, the coded Jth character of C$ is printed out and the program goes on to the next character in A$.

We finish the program with

```
210 PRINT
220 END
```

The complete program is

```
100 DIM A$(72),B$(29),C$(29)
110 LET B$ = "ABCDEFGHIJKLMNOPQRSTUVWXYZ ,."
120 LET C$ = "ETAVZBHCW KPSYDF,GXIMJLONQU.R"
130 INPUT A$
140 FOR I = 1 TO LEN(A$)
150 FOR J = 1 TO 29
160 IF seg(A$,I,I) <> seg(B$,J,J) THEN 190
170 PRINT SEG(C$(J,J);
```

```
180 GOTO 200
190 NEXT J
200 NEXT I
210 PRINT
220 END
```

If your computers numbers strings from zero, lines 140 and 150 should read

```
140 FOR I = 0 TO LEN(A$)
150 FOR J = 0 TO 28
```

The code can be changed by rearranging the characters in C$. It might be interesting for you to try out the program and see how a coded message looks.

8-5 PROBLEMS

1. Write a program to call for the input of a string. Then print the string out in a vertical column of characters.

2. Write a program to call for the input of a string. Then print the string back diagonally down and across the page so that each character is one line below and one character to the right of the previous character.

3. Write a program to count the number of vowels in an input string.

4. Write a program to call for the input of a string. Then print the words in the string in a vertical column.

5. Ask for a sentence to be input. Generate a new string from this sentence that has all the spaces removed. Then print out the new string.

6. Write a program to call for the input of a string consisting of upper-case letters. Then convert all the upper-case letters to lower-case and print the string back. You will need to refer to the ASCII character set in Table 1 in this chapter.

7. Assume that five sentences are to be typed in one at a time. Write a program to count the number of times the word THE appears in the five sentences.

8. If at the input prompt for the program below you type in the string ABCDEFGH what will be output?

```
100 DIM A$(72)
110 INPUT A$
```

```
120 FOR J = 1 TO LEN(A$) STEP 2
130 PRINT se$(A$,J,J);
140 NEXT J
150 END
```

9. Write a program to call for the input of a string. Count the number of times the character I is followed by the character N.

10. We want to count the frequency of occurence of each of the 26 letters in the alphabet (you may assume that they are all upper-case) in ten sentences to be typed in at the keyboard. Do not count spaces or punctuation marks. Write a program to compute and print out a table consisting of each of the letters and the number of times it ocurred in the sentences. Do you think you could identify an author with the use of such a table?

8-6 PRACTICE TEST

Take the following test to see how well you have mastered the chapter. The answers are at the end of the book.

1. How are string variables identified in BASIC?

2. With regard to string variables, what is the purpose of the DIM statement?

3. If A$ = "KITTY" and B$ = "KITTYCAT" then A$ > B$. True or false?

4. If A$ = "HOW NOW BROWN COW" write a function that will extract NOW BROWN.

5. Write a program to call for the input of a string and then keep printing back the string with one character deleted each time until nothing is left. If, for example, you typed in PIECE OF CAKE, the computer should print out

```
PIECE OF CAKE
IECE OF CAKE
ECE OF CAKE
CE OF CAKE
E OF CAKE
 OF CAKE
OF CAKE
F CAKE
 CAKE
CAKE
AKE
KE
E
```

6. What will be printed out if the following program is executed?

```
100 FOR N = 65 TO 90
110 FOR M = 65 TO N
120 PRINT chr$(M);
130 NEXT M
140 PRINT
150 NEXT N
160 END
```

"Do-It-Yourself" Functions and Subroutines

9-1 OBJECTIVES

In this chapter we will learn how the computer can be programmed to perform suboperations. This can be done through either program segments or special on-line instructions. Specifically, we will look at the following things.

"Do-It-Yourself" Functions

We have previously seen functions that are built into BASIC. Now we will learn how to define our own functions to carry out any desired task.

Subroutines

When complicated operations are to be repeated, often subroutines are very useful. We will explore how subroutines can be set up and used in BASIC programs.

Program Applications

Sometimes it is difficult for the beginner to see the value of user-defined functions and subroutines. These ideas will be stressed in our continued attention to programming in BASIC.

228 BASIC: A Hands-on Method

9-2 DISCOVERY EXERCISES

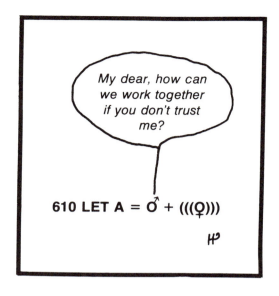

Computer Work

1. Sign on the computer and enter the following program:

```
100 DEF FNA(X) = 5*X+4
110 LET X = 2
120 LET Y = 5*X+4
130 PRINT Y,FNA(2)
140 END
```

Execute the program and record the output below.

---

2. Type

```
130 PRINT Y,FNA(X)
```

"Do-It-Yourself" Functions and Subroutines

Display the program in your work space. What do you think will happen if we execute this program?

_____

Execute the program. What did happen?

3. Type

                110 LET X = 5

Display the program and study it. Now what will be output if we execute the program?

_____

See if you were right. Execute the program and record what happened.

_____

4. Type

                130 PRINT Y,FNA(5)

Display the program. What do you think the program will do now?

_____

Execute the program and write down the output.

_____

5. Notice that the expressions after the equal signs in lines 100 and 120 of your program are the same. In one of the versions of the program, we printed out Y and FNA(X) and saw that they were the same. Let's follow up on this information. Clear out the program in your work space. Then enter the following program:

```
100 DEF FNA(X) = X^2
110 DEF FNB(X) = 3*X
120 DEF FNC(X) = X+2
130 LET X = 1
140 PRINT FNA(X),FNB(X),FNC(X)
150 END
```

Study the program carefully. What do you think will be printed out if the program is executed?

___

Now execute the program and write down what happened.

___

Substitute 1 for X in the expressions on the right side of lines 100, 110, and 120 in your program. Write down the numbers you obtain.

___

Now compare these numbers to those typed out by the computer.

6. Type

$$130 \text{ LET } X = 2$$

Display the program. What will be printed out by the program if it is executed now?

___

"Do-It-Yourself" Functions and Subroutines

See if you were right. Execute the program and record the results below.

_____

7. Type

$$130 \ LET \ X = 3$$

Now what will happen if the program is executed?

_____

Verify your answer by executing the program and recording what happened.

_____

8. Now on to some more ideas we can explore with this program. Type

```
130 LET X = 1
140 PRINT FNC(X+4),FNA(X),FNB(2)
```

Display the program. Write down what you think will be printed out if the program is executed.

_____

Execute the program and record the output.

_____

232   BASIC: A Hands-on Method

9. Let's try a slightly different variation on the theme we have been exploring. Type

140 PRINT FNA(X),FNB(FNA(X))

Display the program and study it carefully. Try to figure out what will be printed out when the progam is executed. Record your answer below.

_____

Execute the program and see if you were right. Write down below what happened.

_____

10. One last point on this matter. Type

130 LET X = 4
140 PRINT FNA(X),FNC(X),FNA(SQR(X))

Now what will happen in the program?

_____

Execute the program and record what happened?

_____

11. Clear out the program in your work space. Enter the following program:

"Do-It-Yourself" Functions and Subroutines   233

```
100 PRINT "A";
110 GOSUB 200
120 PRINT "B";
130 GOSUB 300
140 PRINT "C";
150 STOP
200 PRINT 1;
210 RETURN
300 PRINT 2;
310 RETURN
400 END
```

This program has three new statements that you haven't seen so far. These are GOSUB, RETURN, and STOP. The program itself is intended only to provide practice in tracing these new statements. Execute the program and record the output.

_____

Compare what was printed out with the program lines that caused the printout.

_____

12. The GOSUB statement in line 110 transfers the program to which statement? (Hint: Look at the printout in step 11.)

_____

13. The RETURN statement in line 210 transfers the program to which statement? (Hint: Again, examine the printout in step 11.)

_____

14. The line numbers below indicate the flow of the program as it is executed.

Line Number	What Happens
100	Print out *A*
110	Transfer to line 200
200	Print out 1
210	Transfer to line 120
120	Print out *B*
130	Transfer to line 300
300	Print out *2*
310	Transfer to line 140
140	Print out *C*
150	Transfer to line 400
400	End of program

Study this carefully and follow through with the program. Can you see the purpose of the GOSUB and RETURN statements yet? What about the STOP statement?

15. Clear out the program in your work space. Enter the following program:

```
100 REM PROGRAM TO DEMONSTRATE SUBROUTINES
110 DIM X(4)
120 MAT READ X
130 REM SORT
140 GOSUB 300
150 REM PRINT OUT SORTED ARRAY
160 MAT PRINT X,
170 LET X(3) = 7
180 REM SORT
190 GOSUB 300
200 REM PRINT OUT SORTED ARRAY
210 MAT PRINT X,
220 STOP
300 REM SUBROUTINE TO SORT
310 FOR I = 1 TO 3
320 IF X(I+1) > X(I) THEN 370
330 LET C = X(I+1)
340 LET X(I+1) = X(I)
350 LET X(I) = C
360 GOTO 310
370 NEXT I
380 RETURN
400 DATA 2,1,5,6
500 END
```

"Do-It-Yourself" Functions and Subroutines   **235**

Display the program and check that you have entered it correctly. This program furnishes an example of how a subroutine might be used. The subroutine in lines 300 through 380 sorts the array X into ascending order. Execute the program and record the output.

Note that the original array is

          2   1   5   6

You can see this by checking the DATA statement in line 400. In line 140, the program jumps to the subroutine and a sort of the numbers is done. After the program returns to line 150, the sorted array is now

          1   2   5   6

In line 170, we change the third element of the array, then branch to the subroutine for another sorting. After the return to line 200, the sorted array

          1   2   6   7

is printed out. Finally, the STOP command in line 200 causes the program to jump to the END statement.

Clearly, we could sort the array X as often as desired by merely inserting a statement GOSUB 300. This is certainly more efficient than writing out the instructions for sorting each time it is desired.

16. This completes the computer work for this chapter. Sign off the computer.

236 BASIC: A Hands-on Method

9-3 DISCUSSION

Now we need to examine the ideas introduced in the computer work. Once you understand clearly how the computer handles these ideas, you will have powerful new skills to use in your programs.

Do-It-Yourself Functions

The DEF (an abbreviation for define) statement permits us to have user-specified functions in BASIC programs in addition to those functions (SQR, INT, etc.) already built into the language. The form of all DEF statements is the same.

<line #> DEF FN<letter><variable> = <expression using variable>

100 DEF FNP(X) = X^2-3*X

Since there are twenty-six letters in the alphabet that could follow FN, we could conceivably have twenty-six defined functions in a single program. The variable (e.g.., X in FNP(X)) must appear in the expression on the right side of the equal sign.

If the DEF statement in line 100 were used in a program, and later on the expression FNP(2) were used, the computer would identify that FNP was defined in line 100 and would then substitute 2 for X on the right side of the equal sign in the DEF statement, with the result that

$$FNP(2) = -2$$

Likewise, if T = 5, then

$$FNP(T) = 10$$

The built-in functions in BASIC may be used in the DEF statements. For example,

```
100 DEF FNB(Y) = SQR(Y^1.5)+3*Y
```

is OK. However, if you try to use other defined functions in a DEF statement, you may get into trouble. For example,

```
100 DEF FNB(Y) = FNA(Y) + SQR(Y)
```

may or may not be accepted by your computer. You can discover easily whether it is permissible or not by typing the expression into your computer and seeing what happens.

The primary purpose of the user-specified functions that are set up with the DEF statements is to simplify programming by avoiding repeated use of complicated expressions. The wise programmer should be alert for opportunities to save effort with the use of DEF statements.

Subroutines

One of the limitations of the DEF statements is that only a single variable may be involved and we are limited to a single line. Actually, on some computers this isn't

Define your own functions with a DEF statement.

true, but in this book we will assume that we are bound by these limitations. More complicated situations in which we want to carry out the same process many times in a program are bound to come up. Here is where subroutines are very useful. The diagram below indicates how a subroutine might be used in a program.

```
Main program begins    ─────────────
                       ─────────────
                       ─────────────
                       200    GOSUB 1000
                       210
                       ─────────────
                       ─────────────
                       ─────────────
                       350    GOSUB 1000
                       360
                       ─────────────
                       ─────────────
Main program ends      430    STOP
Subroutine begins      1000   REM SUBROUTINE
                       ─────────────
                       ─────────────
                       ─────────────
End of subroutine      1150   RETURN
End of program         1200   END
```

If the typical program above were executed, when the computer reached the GOSUB in line 200, the program would jump to the beginning of the subroutine in line 1000. The subroutine would be executed, and when the RETURN was encountered in line 1150, control would be passed to the next higher line number after the GOSUB that put us in the subroutine. In this case the program would jump back to line 210. Then the computer would proceed through the main program to the GOSUB in line 350, which would again branch control to the subroutine in line 1000. This time the RETURN would jump back in the program to line 360.

Of course, we could have used GOSUB 1000 as many times as we wanted in the program or could have had as many subroutines as needed. Generally, the top part of the program is the main program and the subroutines are grouped together at the end. There is a good reason for this. We want to perform the subroutines only when they are called by a GOSUB. Thus, after the main program is finshed we put a STOP statement in the program. This is precisely the same as a GOTO the END statement and jumps across all the subroutines grouped together at the end of the program. We can use the STOP statement anywhere there is a logical end to the program. This may occur several times in any given program.

It is possible, and sometimes desirable, to jump to a subroutine from a subroutine. The diagram below indicates how the computer treats such an event.

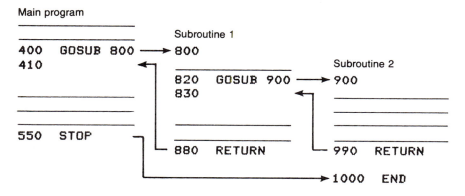

240 BASIC: A Hands-on Method

Note that the control passes from 400 to 800, on down to 820, to 900, and on down to the RETURN in line 990. Of course, the question here is, Does the RETURN take us back to line 410 or line 830? The answer is determined by the rule that the RETURN takes us back to the next statement after the GOSUB that put us in the subroutine containing the RETURN. We are in subroutine 2 because of the GOSUB in line 820; hence the RETURN in line 990 branches us back to line 830. The same rule applies when we reach the RETURN in line 880. At that point we are in subroutine 1 and were put there by the GOSUB in line 400. Thus, the RETURN in line 880 carries us back to line 410. Finally, the STOP statement in line 550 jumps control to the END statement in line 1000.

At this point it may not be clear to you why subroutines are valuable. The need for subroutines becomes more evident as you acquire more skill as a programmer. It is enough at this time to point out that subroutines are extrememly important and are considered to be one of the most powerful tools available to the programmer.

9-4 PROGRAM EXAMPLES

Several programs should assist you to master the ideas involved in both user-defined functions and subroutines.

Example 1—Rounding Off Dollar Values to Cents

Business applications generally involve printing out the results of calculations in dollars and cents. Since the computer usually handles six significant figures, we might get an amount like 23.1579 typed out. This looks strange, and to solve the problem we should round off the figure to the nearest cent, or 23.16.

"Do-It-Yourself" Functions and Subroutines

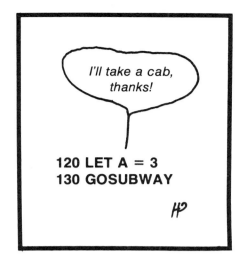

This is an ideal application for a user-defined function. Let's write a program that will produce the following output when executed:

```
LABEL PRICE? (You type in price)
10% DISCOUNT IS (Computer prints discount price)
15% DISCOUNT IS (Computer prints discount price)
20% DISCOUNT IS (Computer prints discount price)
```

All dollar values typed out should be rounded off to the nearest cent.

First we must define a function to do the rounding. Such a function is

```
100 DEF FNR(X) = INT(X*100+.5)/100
```

To see how this rule works, suppose X = 23.1597. We can follow this value through the expression to see what happens.

```
X*100 = 2315.97
X*100+0.5 = 2316.47
INT(X*100+0.5) = 2316
INT(X*100+0.5)/100 = 23.16
```

Therefore 23.1597 was correctly rounded up to 23.16.
As a second example, suppose that X = 23.1547. Then

```
X*100 = 2315.47
X*100+0.5 = 2315.97
INT(X*100+0.5) = 2315
INT(X*100+0.5)/100 = 23.15
```

with the result that 23.1547 was correctly rounded down to 23.15.
The next few lines of the program are self-explanatory.

```
110 PRINT "LABEL PRICE"
120 INPUT Z
130 PRINT "10% DISCOUNT IS";FNR(.9*Z)
140 PRINT "15% DISCOUNT IS";FNR(.85*Z)
150 PRINT "20% DISCOUNT IS";FNR(.8*Z)
```

If desired, we can loop back to the beginning with

```
160 GOTO 110
```

and then end the program.

```
170 END
```

The complete program is

```
100 DEF FNR(X) = INT(X*100+.5)/100
110 PRINT "LABEL PRICE";
120 INPUT Z
130 PRINT "10% DISCOUNT IS";FNR(.9*Z)
140 PRINT "15% DISCOUNT IS";FNR(.85*Z)
150 PRINT "20% DISCOUNT IS";FNR(.8*Z)
160 GOTO 110
170 END
```

In lines 130, 140, and 150 the defined function is used. For a 10 percent discount, the selling price is 90 percent of the original prize Z. Hence, we print out FNR(0.9*Z), which rounds off the value to the nearest cent as desired. Note the economy of using the defined function rather that writing out the expression in line 100 each time we want to print out a rounded dollar amount.

Example 2—Carpet Estimating

We want to write a program that uses a subroutine to compute the price of installed carpet. Suppose that there are four grades of carpet and each is discounted as the quantity of carpet ordered increases. We will assume that the price structure is as follows:

		Price per square yard		
		1	2	3
	A	$10.00	$ 8.50	$ 7.25
Grade	B	13.25	12.00	9.75
	C	16.00	14.00	11.25
	D	20.00	17.20	15.25

1. First 15 square yards

2. Any part of the order exceeding 15 but not more than 25 square yards

3. Anything over 25 square yards

When executed, the program should produce the following output:

```
HOW MANY ROOMS? (You type in)
FOR EACH ROOM, TYPE IN LENGTH
AND WIDTH IN FEET SEPARATED
BY A COMMA

ROOM                DIMENSIONS

1                       (You type in)
2                       (You type in)
        (Loop until all rooms are entered)


   (Computer types out number) SQUARE YARDS REQUIRED
```

244 BASIC: A Hands-on Method

```
CARPET GRADE          COST OF ORDER

A                     (Computer types out,etc.)
B
C
D
```

Before getting involved in the program, we should think a bit about the output. Since the output is in dollars and cents, we may as well use the defined function from Example 1 to take care of rounding off the answers properly. So let's begin the program with that defined function.

```
IN 9.29  100 DEF FNR(X) = INT(X*100+.5)/100
```

The next few lines follow without difficulty.

```
110 PRINT "HOW MANY ROOMS";
120 INPUT N
130 PRINT "FOR EACH ROOM, TYPE IN LENGTH"
140 PRINT "AND WIDTH IN FEET SEPARATED"
150 PRINT "BY A COMMA"
160 PRINT
170 PRINT "ROOM","DIMENSIONS"
180 PRINT
```

Now we are ready to call for the input of the room dimensions. We will use the variable A to keep track of the area of the rooms. Remember that the area of a room is its length times its width.

```
190 LET A = 0
200 FOR I = 1 TO N
210 PRINT I,
220 INPUT L,W
230 LET A = A+L*W
240 NEXT I
```

Since the total room area is now in square feet, we must divide this by 9 to convert to square yards, and then we will print out the quantity of carpet required.

```
250 LET A = A/9
260 PRINT A;"SQUARE YARDS REQUIRED"
```

"Do-It-Yourself" Functions and Subroutines **245**

At this point we may as well include the price table in the program in the form of DATA statements.

```
270 DATA 10,8.5,7.25
280 DATA 13.25,12,9.75
290 DATA 16,14,11.25
300 DATA 20,17.2,15.25
```

Next we can print out the heading required for the price printout.

```
310 PRINT
320 PRINT "CARPET GRADE","COST OF ORDER"
330 PRINT
```

Now we come to the point in the program where the subroutine will be useful. Since we don't know precisely where the subroutine should begin, we will simply use a large line number and correct it later if needed.

```
340 REM COMPUTE PRICE FOR GRADE A
350 GOSUB 800
```

Let's write the subroutine now. First, for each of the grades of carpet we need the three prices. We can do this by reading them from the DATA statements.

```
800 REM SUBROUTINE TO COMPUTE CARPET PRICE
810 READ C1,C2,C3
```

Next check to see if the area of the carpet is less that 15, between 15 and 25, or more than 25 square yards and then compute the price accordingly.

```
820 IF A > 25 THEN 860
830 IF A > 15 THEN 880
840 LET P = C1*A
850 GOTO 890
860 LET P = 15*C1 + 10*C2 + (A-25)*C3
870 GOTO 890
880 LET P = 15*C1 + (A-15)*C2
890 RETURN
```

Trace this program segment through to convince yourself that the price is being computed correctly. Now we can return to the main program and print out the first price.

```
360 PRINT "A",FNR(P)
```

Once this pattern has been established, the rest of the main program follows easily.

```
370 REM COMPUTE PRICE FOR GRADE B
380 GOSUB 800
390 PRINT "B",FNR(P)
400 REM COMPUTE PRICE FOR GRADE C
410 GOSUB 800
420 PRINT "C",FNR(P)
430 REM COMPUTE PRICE FOR GRADE D
440 GOSUB 800
450 PRINT "D",FNR(P)
460 STOP
```

The STOP statement in line 460 is needed to prevent the program from falling into the subroutine. The value of the subroutine becomes clear when we see that had it not been available, each of the four GOSUB statements would have had to be replaced with as many statements as in the subroutine.

The complete program is

```
100 DEF FNR(X) = INT(X*100+.5)/100
110 PRINT "HOW MANY ROOMS"
120 INPUT N
130 PRINT "FOR EACH ROOM, TYPE IN LENGTH"
140 PRINT "AND WIDTH IN FEET SEPARATED"
150 PRINT "BY A COMMA"
160 PRINT
170 PRINT "ROOM","DIMENSIONS"
180 PRINT
190 LET A = 0
200 FOR I = 1 TO N
210 PRINT I,
220 INPUT L,W
230 LET A = A+L*W
240 NEXT I
250 LET A = A/9
260 PRINT A;"SQUARE YARDS REQUIRED"
270 DATA 10,8.5,7.25
280 DATA 13.25,12,9.75
290 DATA 16,14,11.25
300 DATA 20,17.2,15.25
```

```
310 PRINT
320 PRINT "CARPET GRADE","COST OF ORDER"
330 PRINT
340 REM COMPUTE PRICE FOR GRADE A
350 GOSUB 800
360 PRINT "A",FNR(P)
370 REM COMPUTE PRICE FOR GRADE B
380 GOSUB 800
390 PRINT "B",FNR(P)
400 REM COMPUTE PRICE FOR GRADE C
410 GOSUB 800
420 PRINT "C",FNR(P)
430 REM COMPUTE PRICE FOR GRADE D
440 GOSUB 800
450 PRINT "D",FNR(P)
460 STOP
800 REM SUBROUTINE TO COMPUTE CARPET PRICE
810 READ C1,C2,C3
820 IF A > 25 THEN 860
830 IF A > 15 THEN 880
840 LET P = C1*A
850 GOTO 890
860 LET P = 15*C1 + 10*C2 + (A-25)*C3
870 GOTO 890
880 LET P = 15*C1 + (A-15)*C2
890 RETURN
900 END
```

9-5 PROBLEMS

1. Trace the program below and write down what will be printed out if the program is executed.

```
100 DEF FNA(X) = 2+X
110 DEF FNB(Y) = 10*Y
120 DEF FNC(Z) = Z^2
130 LET R = 2
140 LET S = 3
150 LET T = 5
160 PRINT FNC(T),FNA(S),FNB(R)
170 LET R = S+T
180 PRINT FNA(R) + FNB(S) + FNC(T)
190 END
```

2. What will be printed out if the program below is executed?

```
100 DEF FNX(A) = 6*A
110 DEF FNY(B) = B+10
120 DEF FNZ(C) = C^3
130 READ P,Q,R
140 DATA 1,2,3
150 PRINT FNX(R),FNZ(P),FNY(Q)
160 PRINT FNY(P+Q) + FNX(R)
170 END
```

3. The area of a circle is Pi times R squared, and the volume of a sphere is 4/3 times Pi times R cubed. Pi is 3.14159, and R is either the radius of the circle or the radius of the sphere. Define two DEF statements, one for the circle and one for the sphere. Set up a FOR NEXT loop on R for R from 1 to 10 in steps of 0.5. Use the defined functions to print out a table of areas and volumes for each of the values of R.

4. What will be output by the following program if it is executed?

```
100 DIM A(5)
110 MAT READ A
120 DATA 6,2,7,1,3
130 GOSUB 500
140 MAT PRINT A,
150 LET A(3) = 10
160 GOSUB 500
```

"Do-It-Yourself" Functions and Subroutines

```
170 MAT PRINT A,
180 LET A(5) = 8
190 GOSUB 500
200 MAT PRINT A,
210 STOP
500 FOR I = 1 TO 4
510 LET A(I) = A(I+1)
520 NEXT I
530 RETURN
600 END
```

5. What will be printed out if the program below is executed?

```
100 LET X = 10
110 GOSUB 500
120 PRINT S
130 LET X = X/2
140 GOSUB 500
150 PRINT S
160 LET X = X+3
170 GOSUB 500
180 PRINT S
190 STOP
500 LET S = 0
510 FOR Y = 1 TO X
520 LET S = S+Y
530 NEXT Y
540 RETURN
600 END
```

6. Assume that a one-dimensional array Z contains numbers to be added togther. The first element of the array Z(1) gives the number of elements that follow in the array and are to be summed. Write a subroutine beginning in line 800 to compute the sum of the elements after Z(1). Assign the sum to the variable T. Terminate the subroutine with a RETURN statements. Assume that the array Z has been properly dimensioned and that the values in the array have been loaded in the main program.

7. X is a one-dimensional array. The first element of the array X(1) gives the number of pieces of data that follow in the array. Write a subroutine beginning in line 500 to search through that array for the largest value. Assign this value to the variable L. Terminate the subroutine with a RETURN statement. Assume that the array X has been properly dimensioned and loaded with numbers elsewhere.

250 BASIC: A Hands-on Method

8. Suppose that as part of a printout we need a series of seventy-two characters in a straight line across the page. Write a subroutine beginning in line 1000 to do this. Terminate the subroutine with a RETURN statement.

9. Assume that a one-dimensional array Y is loaded with numbers. The first element Y(1) gives the number of elements to follow. We want a subroutine to calcuate the mean (M) and standard deviation (S) of the numbers in the array which follow the first element. Begin the subroutine in line 900 and terminate with a RETURN statement. The formulas for calculation of the mean and standard deviation are given below.

$$\text{Mean} = \text{Sum of values} / N$$

$$\text{Standard deviation} = \sqrt{\frac{N \times (\text{sum of squares of values}) - (\text{sum of values})^2}{N \times (N-1)}}$$

9-6 PRACTICE TEST

Check your progress with the following practice test. The answers are given at the end of the book.

1. If DEF FNA(X) = SQR(X)+3*X, Z = 2.5, and W = 10, what is

   a.   FNA(1)

   b. FNA(4)

   c. FNA(9)

   d. FNA(Z*W)

2. What will be printed out if we execute the following program?

```
100 DEF FNR(X) = X*X
110 DEF FNS(X) = 3*X
120 DEF FNT(Y) = Y+1
130 LET A = 1
140 PRINT FNT(A),FNR(A),FNS(A)
150 LET M = 4
160 PRINT FNR(SQR(M))
170 END
```

3. With regards to subroutines

   a. How do you pass control from the main program to the subroutine?

   _____

   b. How do you pass control from the subroutine back to the main program?

   _____

   c. What is the purpose of the STOP statement?

   _____

4. What will be printed out if we execute the following program?

```
100 LET A = 1
110 GOSUB 200
120 LET A = A+4
130 GOSUB 200
140 LET A = A-2
150 GOSUB 200
160 STOP
200 REM SUBROUTINE
210 IF A < 2 THEN 250
220 IF A = 3 THEN 270
```

```
230 PRINT "RED"
240 GOTO 280
250 PRINT "WHITE"
260 GOTO 280
270 PRINT "BLUE"
280 RETURN
900 END
```

10
Random Numbers and Simulations

10-1 OBJECTIVES

One of the most interesting applications of computers concerns simulation of events or processes that involve an element of chance. Examples might be using the computer to simulate gambling games or perhaps investigating the number of bank tellers required to ensure that arriving customers do not have to wait more than a few minutes to be served. In this chapter we will see how the computer can be used to handle problems of this type. Our objectives are as follows.

Characteristics of Randon-Number Generators

Computers have a random-number generator function that is the heart of all programs involving the element of chance, or randomness. We will learn how these random-number generators can be employed in BASIC programs.

Random Numbers with Special Characteristics

Generally, the random-number generator is used to produce sets of random numbers with characteristics specified by the programmer. We will see how this is done and how any desired set of numbers can be generated.

Programming and Simulations

The programming exercises and problems in this chapter will involve simulations and applications that involve the element of chance.

10-2 DISCOVERY EXERCISES

Setting Up The Random-number Generator.

Before beginning the computer work, we must discuss some important characteristics of random-number generators. By their very nature, these generators produce sequences of numbers that appear to have no pattern or relationship. For a random-number generator to be useful, each time we execute a program that utilizes it we should get a different sequence of numbers. However, this gives rise to an interesting question. Suppose a program that uses random numbers is not working correctly. If the problem is connected with the random numbers it might be extrememly difficult to correct since different random numbers are generated each time the program is executed. Consequently, provisions are always included so that a sequence of random numbers can be repeated each time the program is executed. Remember, though, that this feature of BASIC should be used only when you are trouble-shooting a program. Refer to Appendix A to find out how the random-number generator on your computer can be set to produce either the same or different sequences of numbers each time the program is executed. Record this information below for your future reference.

TO GET A DIFFERENT SEQUENCE OF RANDOM NUMBERS EACH TIME THE PROGRAM IS EXECUTED, DO THE FOLLOWING:_____

Random Numbers and Simulations **255**

TO GET THE SAME SEQUENCE OF RANDOM NUMBERS EACH TIME THE PROGRAM IS EXECUTED, DO THE FOLLOWING: _____

_____

_____

Computer Work

1. Sign on the computer. Unless otherwise specified, assume that different sequences of numbers are to be generated each time a program is executed. This requirement may require an additional statement in the programs, depending on the computer you are using.

2. Enter the following program:

```
100 FOR I = 1 TO 10
110 PRINT RND(0)
120 NEXT I
130 END
```

Execute the program and record the largest and smallest numbers that were printed out.

_____

3. Execute the program again. Did the same numbers appear?

_____

What was the largest number typed out?

_____

256 BASIC: A Hands-on Method

What was the smallest number?

_____

4. Clear out the program in your work space and enter the following program:

```
100 LET L = .5
110 LET S = .5
120 FOR I = 1 TO 100
130 LET X = RND(0)
140 IF X > L THEN 170
150 IF X < S THEN 190
160 GOTO 200
170 LET L = X
180 GOTO 200
190 LET S = X
200 NEXT I
210 PRINT "LARGEST = ";L
220 PRINT "SMALLEST = ";S
230 END
```

This program examines all the numbers generated by the RND function and keeps track of the largest and smallest numbers generated. As the program stands, it will generate 100 random numbers. Execute the program and record what was typed out.

_____

5. Type

```
120 FOR I = 1 TO 1000
```

Now the program will generate 1000 random numbers. Execute the program and record what was printed out.

_____

Based upon what you have seen thus far, what do you believe is the largest number that will be generated by the RND function?

___

What about the smallest?

___

6. Now let's go on to some other ideas associated with random numbers. Clear out the program in your work space and enter the following program:

```
100 FOR I = 1 TO 10
110 PRINT INT(2*RND(0))
120 NEXT I
130 END
```

Execute the program and record the output.

___

What were the only two numbers typed out?

___

7. Type

```
110 PRINT INT(3*RND(0))
```

Display the program. If this program is executed, what numbers do you think will be typed out?

___

258 BASIC: A Hands-on Method

Can you predict anything about the sequence or pattern in which the numbers wil be typed out?

_____

8. Type

   110 PRINT INT(2*RND(0)+1)

What do you think the program will do now?

_____

Execute the program and record the output.

_____

9. Type

   110 PRINT INT(4*RND(0)+4)

If the program is executed, what do you think will be printed out?

_____

Execute the program and describe the output.

_____

Random Numbers and Simulations

Any pattern to the output?

___

10. Type

```
110 PRINT INT(30*RND(0))/10
```

Display the program and study it carefully. What do you think this program will print out?

___

Execute the program and describe the printout.

___

11. Type

```
110 PRINT INT(200*RND(0))/100
```

Display the program in your work space. What do you think will happen if this program is executed?

___

See if you were right. Execute the program and record the output below.

___

260 BASIC: A Hands-on Method

12. Sign off the computer. This terminates the computer work for now.

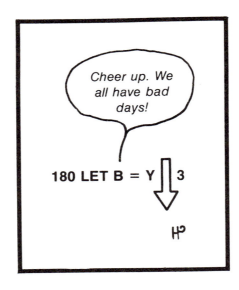

10-3 DISCUSSION

Now that you have seen some of the characteristics of the random-number generator on the computer, we can profitably proceed to a complete discussion of the matter.

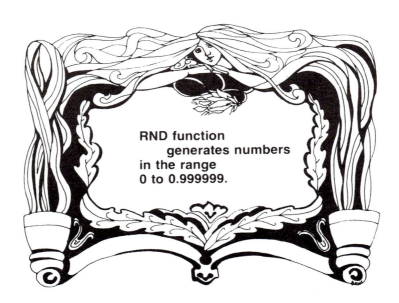

Random-Number Generators

We will not become involved with the details of how random numbers are generated. It is enough to say that there are several mathematical methods to produce these numbers. Different manufacturers use different methods. The random-number generator is called on with the RND function. This function is used like the other built-in functions in BASIC that were studied previously, but differs in two important respects. Recall that the argument of a function (what the function works on) determines the result. Thus. SQR(4) is 2, INT(3.456) is 3, and so forth. However the argument of the RND function has no effect on the numbers produced. This statement isn't completely true but is close enough to the truth for the point that needs to be made. If you use(RND(0) or RND(3) or RND(238) in a program, all will have precisely the same effect. As a matter of fact, a variable can be used as the argument of the RND function. RND(Z) is all right provided that Z has been defined somewhere else in the program. So this is the first major difference in the RND function as compared with the others we have studied. The argument has no effect on the function and consequently is known as a "dummy argument". A good rule of thumb is to use 0 as the argument of the RND functions.

The second major difference is that there seems to be no pattern or rule used in generating numbers with the RND function. Of course, this is precisely the point of the function. RND stands for "random." The function generates numbers between 0 and 1 at random. All the numbers in the interval have an equal chance of showing up. Actually, the range of numbers generated is from 0.000000 to 0.999999. Zero can show up occasionally, but the number 1 never occurs.

Designing Sets of Random Numbers

Most often we do not want random numbers in the range produced by the RND function. We might want random integers (whole numbers) over a certain range or a set of random numbers with a particular set of characteristics. Therefore, we must give some thought to how to generate sets of random numbers with characteristics we can specify.

Let's begin with the characteristics of the RND function. RND(0) delivers numbers in the range 0 to 1, that is, from 0 to slightly less than 1. If we multiply RND(0) by N, we multiply the range of the function by N. Thus, N*RND(0) will produce random numbers in the range 0 to N. If desired, we could shift the numbers (keeping the same range) by adding a number. N*RND(0)+A would produce random numbers over the range A to (A+N) or from A to slightly less than (A+N). Finally, if desired, we could take the integer part of an expression, using the INT function, to produce random integers. The examples below indicate how the RND function might be used.

BASIC Expression	Result
5*RND(0) + 10	Random numbers in the range 10 to 15
INT(5*RND(0)+10)	Random integers 10,11,12,13,14
INT(2*RND(0)+1)	Random integers 1,2
100*RND(0)	Random numbers in the range 0 to 100

In your studies you may have encountered the notion of mean and standard deviation (see problem 9 in Chapter 9). We can use the RND function to generate numbers that appear to be drawn from a collection of numbers having a given mean and standard deviation. The rule for generating these numbers is

```
X = M + S((sum of 12 numbers from RND function)-6)
```

where M and S are the desired mean and standard deviation, respectively. This is an application in which a subroutine would be very useful. As defined above, the values of X will appear to be coming from a collection of numbers with mean M and standard deviation S. The values of X can be used to simulate a process following the bell curve that you have probably seen in textbooks.

Troubleshooting Programs that Use Random Numbers

We have already pointed out that BASIC provides a way to execute a program several times and repeat the sequence of random numbers that are generated by the RND function. It is usually wise to write programs initially so that they do generate the same sequence of random numbers each time they are executed. Once you are sure that the program is working correctly, you can modify the program to produce the randomness that is the central idea in the RND function.

10-4 PROGRAM EXAMPLES

Now we will go through several examples to illustrate how random numbers can be used. Study these examples carefully and make sure you understand exactly what is taking place.

Example 1 - Flipping Coins

One of the easiest applications of random numbers is a coin-tossing simulation. We want to write a program that when executed will produce the following printout:

```
TOSS           OUTCOME

1              H
2              T
3              T
4              H
         etc.
```

The outcome is to be determined randomly for each toss of the coin, with both heads and tails having equal probability. The program should print out the results of ten coin tosses.

The first part of the program generates the heading and the space indicated in the printout above.

```
100 PRINT "TOSS","OUTCOME"
110 PRINT
```

Now we must open the loop to generate the ten tosses of the coin.

```
120 FOR I = 1 TO 10
```

The next step is to generate 0s and 1s randomly. We will assume that the occurrence of a 0 means a "head" and the occurrence of a 1 means a "tail". You should be able to convince yourself that the following statement will produce 0s and 1s randomly.

```
130 LET X = INT(2*RND(0))
```

Now we analyze X to see whether a head (0) or a tail (1) has occurred.

```
140 IF X = 0 THEN 170
150 PRINT I,"T"
160 GOTO 180
170 PRINT I,"H"
180 NEXT I
```

264 BASIC: A Hands-on Method

All that remains now is the END statement.

```
190 END
```

The complete program is listed below.

```
100 PRINT "TOSS","OUTCOME"
110 PRINT
120 FOR I = 1 TO 10
130 LET X = INT(2*RND(0))
140 IF X = 0 THEN 170
150 PRINT I,"T"
160 GOTO 180
170 PRINT I,"H"
180 NEXT I
190 END
```

This is a good program for demonstrating how the computer can be instructed to produce either different sequences of random numbers or identical sequences each time the program is executed. Make the necessary changes in the program to see this work.

Example 2 – Random Integers

The next problem is to write a BASIC program to generate and print out fifty random integers (whole numbers) over the range 10 to 15. The only part of the program that will require much thought is the statement to generate the random integers, so we will concentrate on this one statement.

Remember that RND(0) generates numbers over the range 0 to 1. Thus, 6*RND(0) will generate numbers in the range 0 to 6. Actually the upper limit is 5.99999. By using the integer function we can convert from random numbers to random integers. INT(6*RND(0)) will produce the integers 0, 1, 2, 3, 4, 5 randomly. Now it is clear that to get the desired numbers, we must add 10. Thus, the expression INT(6*RND(0)) + 10 will produce the numbers we want.

Once we have this one line figured out, the program follows easily.

```
100 FOR I = 1 TO 50
110 LET Y = INT(6*RND(0)) + 10
120 PRINT Y,
130 NEXT I
140 END
```

Example 3 – Distribution of Random Numbers

Suppose we generate a great number of integers at random over the range 1 to 10. If the random-number generator on the computer is working the way it should, we would expect to get the same number of each of the integers. If we generated 10,000 integers, we would expect to get 1000 1s, 1000 2s, and so on. Our problem will be to write a BASIC program to do a tally of the random integers as they are generated and then print out the totals. Inspection of these totals will tell us how good the random-number generator on the computer really is.

First let's think about how we are going to do the tally. A good way to do this is to use a one-dimensional subscripted array. X(1) will contain the number of 1s generated, X(2) the number of 2s, and so forth on up to X(10). Thus, the first task is to dimension the array and set all the values in the array equal to 0.

```
100 DIM X(10)
110 MAT X = ZER
```

Next we open a loop to generate 10,000 numbers, generate the random integers, then use the integers as subscipts to increment the appropriate counters in the array.

```
120 FOR I = 1 TO 10000
130 LET Y = INT(10*RND(0)) + 1
140 LET X(Y) = X(Y) + 1
150 NEXT I
```

Now all that remains is to print out the contents of the array X.

```
160 FOR J = 1 TO 10
170 PRINT J,X(J)
180 NEXT J
190 END
```

The complete program follows:

```
100 DIM X(10)
110 MAT X = ZER
120 FOR I = 1 TO 10000
130 LET Y = INT(10*RND(0)) + 1
140 LET X(Y) = X(Y) + 1
150 NEXT I
```

266 BASIC: A Hands-on Method

```
160 FOR J = 1 TO 10
170 PRINT J,X(J)
180 NEXT J
190 END
```

It might be interesting for you to execute this program and see for youself how the random-number generator on your computer checks out. If you decrease the number of integers generated, the agreement between what you expect and what actually takes place should get worse. On the other hand, if you generate more random numbers, the agreement should get better.

Example 4 – Birthday Pairs in a Crowd

Suppose that fifty strangers get together in a room. What is the probability that two of the people have the same birthday? We consider only the day of the year, not the year of birth. This problem is a famous one in probability theory and has surprising results. We can attack the problem with the following strategy. By generating random integers over the range 1 to 365, we can simulate a birthday for each of the strangers. If we use a one-dimensional array for the birthdays as they are generated, it is easy to check for identical birthdays. Beginning with the first birthday B(1), we check to see if it matches any of the remaining ones. Then we do the same thing for B(2), and so on.

For this example, we will depart from the usual method and will look at the complete program; then go back over the details.

```
100 DIM B(50)
110 FOR I = 1 TO 50
120 LET B(I) = INT(365*RND(0)) + 1
130 NEXT I
140 LET F = 0
150 FOR I = 1 TO 49
160 FOR J = I+1 TO 50
170 IF B(I) <> B(J) THEN 190
180 LET F = F + 1
190 NEXT J
200 NEXT I
210 PRINT "NUMBER OF BIRTHDAY PAIRS FOUND IS";F
220 END
```

Of course, line 100 merely dimensions an array for fifty elements. Lines 110 through 130 load the array with random integers selected over the range 1 to 365 inclusive. In line 140, we set the variable F equal to 0. We will use this variable to keep track of the number of birthdays that will be compared with the rest of the birthdays in the list. Since there must be at least one birthday left in the list to compare with, the value of I stops at 49. In line 160, the second half of the comparison is set up.

Random Numbers and Simulations 267

J begins at the next value past the current value of I and runs through the rest of the list. The test for a birthday pair is made in line 170. If no match if found, we jump to the next value of J. If a match is found, the pair counter is increased by 1 in line 180. The results are printed out in line 210. One problem with the program is that it would record three people having the same birthday as two birthday pairs. Can you figure out a way to fix this?

This is a very interesting program to experiment with. The number of the people in the crowd can be modified with simple changes in the program. The program can be executed many times to see how many birthday pairs on the average will be found in a crowd of a specified size.

10-5 PROBLEMS

1. Write a program to generate and print out twenty-five random numbers of the form X.Y where X and Y are digits selected randomly from the set 0, 1, 2, 3...4.

2. Write a program to generate and print out fifty integers selected at random from the range 13 to 25.

3. What will be printed out if the following program is executed?

```
100 FOR N = 1 TO 20
110 PRINT INT(20*RND(0)+1)/100
120 NEXT N
130 END
```

4. If the following program is executed, what will be printed out?

```
100 FOR I = 1 TO 10
110 PRINT INT(100*RND(0))/10
120 NEXT I
130 END
```

5. Write a program that will simulate tossing a coin, 10, 50, 500, and 1000 times. In each case, print out the total number of heads and tails that occur.

6. Construct a dice-throwing simulation in BASIC. The dice are to be thrown twenty times. For each toss, print out the dice faces that are uppermost.

7. Write a program to generate and print out the average of 100 random numbers selected from the range 0 to 1.

8. Modify the program of Example 4 and execute it as many times as needed to find the size of crowd such that there is a 50 percent chance that at least two people in the crowd have the same birthday.

9. John and Bill want to meet at the library. Each agrees to arrive at the library sometime between 1 and 2 P.M. They further agree that they will wait 10 minutes after arriving (but not after 2 P.M.), and if the other person has not arrived, will leave. Write a BASIC program to compute the probability that John and Bill will meet one another. Do a simulation of the problem using the random-number generator.

10. Suppose a basket contains colored golf balls. There are ten red balls, five blue, two green, and eleven yellow. Write a BASIC program to simulate drawing five balls at random from the bucket if they are not replaced after being drawn in sequence.

11. Use the rule given in the discussion section in this chapter to generate and print out twenty-five numbers selected at random from a bell curve distribution of numbers with mean 10 and standard deviation 2. Round off the numbers to two places past the decimal point.

12. Suppose a soap manufacturer decides to select a five character brand name. The first, third, and fifth characters are selected at random from the letters BCDFGHJKLMNPQRSTVWXYZ. The second and fourth letters are selected at random from the vowels AEIOU. Write a program to generate and print out one hundred trial soap names using the rules above.

13. Modify the program from problem 6 to simulate tossing a pair of dice 1000 times. Print out the number of times each of the eleven possible outcomes happened in the simulation.

14. If it is clear today, there is a 40% chance it will be clear tomorrow; a 30% chance of overcast weather, and a 30% chance of rain. If it is overcast today, there is a 10% chance it will be clear tomorrow, a 30% chance of continued overcast, and a 60% chance of rain. Finally if it is raining today, there is a 60% chance it will be clear tomorrow, a 10% chance of being overcast, and a 30% chance of continued rain. Write a program to print out ten six-day weather cycles according to the probability rules above.

10-6 PRACTICE TEST

Take the following test to see how you are progressing. The answers are given at the end of the book.

1. Write a BASIC program to generate and print out 100 random integers selected from the set 1, 2, 3, and 4.

2. Write a BASIC program to generate and print out 100 random numbers over the range 25 to 50.

3. What wil be printed out if we execute the following program?

```
100 FOR I = 1 TO 10
110 LET N = INT(2*RND(0)+1)
120 IF N = 1 THEN 150
130 PRINT "WHITE"
140 GOTO 160
150 PRINT "RED"
160 NEXT I
170 END
```

4. What will be printed out if we execute the following program?

```
100 FOR J = 1 TO 5
110 PRINT INT(1000*RND(0))/100
120 NEXT J
130 END
```

APPENDIX A
Computer System Commands

Specific instructions for several time-sharing computers are contained in this section. A word of caution is in order. The instructions given here were correct at the time of publication; however, manufacturers often change the operating systems, and changes may have an effect on the instructions. If problems come up, take the blank form in A-22 to your computer center to be filled out.

When using Appendix A, identify the computer manufacturer and model on the list of computers in A-1. It will save time if you go through the rest of the sections and circle the letter corresponding to the computer you will be using. This will make it easier to look up specific commands later. If your computer is not listed in A-1, have the blank form in A-22 filled out at your computer center.

Some details should be kept in mind when using the instructions. Angled brackets (e.g., < >) enclose material to be typed in, but are *not* part of the input. Where spaces must be included they are indicated with the ∧ character. A superscript c (e.g., X^c) means to hold down the CONTROL or CTRL key on the terminal while typing the character. When you are through typing material, press the CARRIAGE RETURN or END OF LINE on the terminal.

A-1 COMPUTER LIST

A   BASIC Time Sharing (System 4000)
B   Data General Corporation (RDOS operating system)
C   Digital Equipment Corporation (RSTS-E, BASIC Plus, System 11/34 to 11/74)
D   Digital Equipment Corporation (System 10, TOPS operating system)
E   Digital Equipment Corporation (System 20, TOPS/20 operating system)
F   Harris (Vulcan operating system)
G   Hewlett Packard 2000 C, E, or F
H   Hewlett Packard 2000 Access
I   Hewlett Packard 3000
J   Honeywell (Data Net Services)

Appendix A — Computer Systems Commands **271**

K   Univac (1100 series)
L   Xerox (Sigma 5-9 series, CP-5 operating system)

A-2 SIGN-ON INSTRUCTIONS

Computer	Instructions
A	Turn on terminal. Press ESCAPE key. System will type /. Then type HELLO-<account number>, <password>.
B	Turn on terminal. Press ESCAPE key. Computer responds with ACCOUNT ID;. Type in <4 digit ID>. Computer responds with information line. At the * prompt the system is ready.
C	Turn on terminal. Type HELLO. The computer types information line, then prints #. Type in <project number>, <programmer number>. Computer comes back with PASSWORD. Type in <password>. System is then ready.
D	Turn on terminal. Type LOGIN. The computer types information line, then prints #. Type in <project number>, <programmer number>. Computer comes back with PASSWORD. Type <password>. The system will respond with a · prompt. Type BASIC. The system prints out READY.
E	Turn on terminal. Type C^c. Computer types out information line. Type LOGIN and press the ESC or ESCAPE key. The computer will respond with USER. Type <user name> and press ESC key. The computer will then type PASSWORD. Type in <password> and press ESC key. System comes back with account #. Type in <account number>. When the system types out @, type in BASIC.
F	Turn on terminal. Type <account #, user ID>. When the terminal advances a line, type BASIC.
G	Turn on terminal. Type HELLO-<account number>, <password>. Computer comes back with information line and ends with READY.
H	Turn on terminal. Press CARRIAGE RETURN and LINEFEED keys. Computer comes back with PLEASE LOG IN. Type HELLO-<account number>, <password> Computer types information line and ends with READY.
I	Turn on terminal. Press RETURN key. Type HELLO ^ <log on ID>. System responds with information line. At the : prompt, type BASIC. At the > prompt, the system is in BASIC and ready.
J	Turn on terminal. Press RETURN. Computer types out information line and then requests user's ID code. Type in <user ID code>. System then requests password. Type in <password>. The computer types out additional information and ends with SYSTEM?. Type

BASIC. The system responds with OLD OR NEW. Type NEW. At the * prompt the system is ready.

K   Turn on terminal. Type @RUN ^<account number>. System types out information line. Type @BASIC. At the > prompt the system is ready.

L   Turn on terminal. Press BREAK key. Computer types out message ending with LOGON PLEASE:. Type <account number>,<name>. Computer comes back with information line. At the : prompt, type BASIC. At the > prompt the system is ready.

A-3 SIGN-OFF INSTRUCTIONS

Computer	Instructions
A,B,C,D,E,G,H,J	Type BYE
F	Type BYE and after information line is typed out type $OFF.
I	Type EXIT and at the : prompt type BYE.
K	Type @FIN.
L	Press BREAK or ESC key four times. At the ! prompt type OFF.

A-4 DISPLAY THE PROGRAM IN WORK SPACE

Computer	Instructions
All	Type LIST.

A-5 EXECUTE THE PROGRAM IN WORK SPACE

Computer	Instructions
All	Type RUN.

A-6 CLEAR OUT THE PROGRAM IN WORK SPACE

Computer	Instructions
A	Type SCR.
B,C,D,E,J,K	Type NEW.
F	Type ELIMINATE-<program name>.
G,H,I	Type SCRATCH.
L	Type CLEAR.

Appendix A — Computer Systems Commands

A-7 JUMP OUT OF AN INPUT LOOP

Computer	Instructions
A,C,D,E,G	Type C^c.
B	Press ESC key.
F	Type S^c.
H,J,L	Press BREAK key.
I	Type Y^c and at the > prompt type ABORT.
K	Type STOP.

A-8 INTERRUPT A RUNNING PROGRAM

Computer	Instructions
A	Press BREAK key twice.
B	Press ESC key.
C	Type C^c.
D,E	Type $C^c C^c$.
G,H,J,L	Press BREAK key.
I	Type Y^c and at the > prompt type ABORT.
K	Press BREAK key, and after message is typed out type @@ ^ CO.

A-9 DELETE A CHARACTER WHILE TYPING

Computer	Instructions
A,F,G	Press ← key.
B,C,D,E,L	Press RUBOUT or DELETE key.
H,I	Type H^c.
J	Type @.
K	Type Z^c.

A-10 DELETE AN ENTIRE LINE WHILE TYPING

Computer	Instructions
A	Press ESCAPE key.
B	Type shift-L.

274 BASIC: A Hands-on Method

C,D,E	Type U^c.
F	Press RUBOUT or DELETE key.
G,H,J,I,K,L	Type X^c.

A-11 RESPOND TO SYSTEM ERROR MESSAGES

Computer	Instructions
A,B,C,D,E,F, G,J,K,L	Computer types out error diagnostic and returns to BASIC.
H,I	Computer prints ERROR and halts. If you want a diagnostic, type any character and then press the RETURN key. If not, simply press the RETURN Key.

A-12 MOVE A PROGRAM FROM MEMORY TO WORK SPACE

Computer	Instructions
A,G,H	Type GET-<program name>.
B	Type LOAD ^<"program name">.
C,D,E,J	Type OLD ^<program name>.
F	Type KEY 0 (a zero) then OLD ^<program name>.
I	Type GET ^<program name>.
K	Type OLD:<program name>.
L	Type LOAD ^ <program name>.

A-13 MOVE A PROGRAM FROM WORK SPACE TO MEMORY

Computer	Instructions
A,C,D,E,G,H, I,J,K	Type SAVE.
B	Type SAVE ^<"program name">.
F	Type SAVE ^ <program name>.
L	Type SAVE ON ^ <program name>.

A-14 CLEAR OUT A PROGRAM IN MEMORY

Computer	Instructions
A,G	Type KILL-<program name>.
B	Type DELETE ^<"program name">.
C,D,E,F	Type UNSAVE ^ <program name>.
H	Type PURGE-<program name>
I,J	Type PURGE ^ <program name>
K	Type UNSAVE:<program name>.
L	Type DELETE ^ <program name>.

A-15 NAME A PROGRAM IN WORK SPACE

Computer	Instructions
A,G,H	Type NAME-<program name>.
B,F	Not used. Program is named when using the SAVE command.
C,D,E,J	Type RENAME ^ <program name>.
I,L	Type NAME ^ <program name>.
K	Type RENAME:<program name>.

A-16 DISPLAY A CATALOG OF PROGRAMS IN ACCOUNT

Computer	Instructions
A,G,H,I,K	Type CAT.
B	Type FILES.
C,D,E,J,L	Type CATALOG.
F	Type MA.GU.

A-17 MTH THROUGH NTH CHARACTERS OF STRING A$

Computer	Instructions
A	A$(M:N)
B,F,J	Unknown
C,D,E	MID(A$,M,N)
G,H,I	A$(M,N)
L	A$(:M,N-M+1)
K	CPY$(A$,M,N-M+1)

A-18 CONVERT POSITION NUMBER TO CORRESPONDING CHARACTER IN ASCII SET

Computer	Instructions
A,C,D,E,H,I	CHR$(N)
B,F,J,K	Unknown.
G	Not available on computer
L	CHAR(N)

A-19 CONVERT CHARACTER TO EQUIVALENT POSITION NUMBER IN ASCII SET

Computer	Instructions
A	ASC(A$)
B,F,J,K	Unknown.
C,D,E	ASCII(A$)
G	Not available on computer.
H,I	NUM(A$)
L	CHAR(A$)

A-20 PRODUCE A DIFFERENT SEQUENCE OF RANDOM NUMBERS

Computer	Instructions
A,G,H,I	Use RND(0).
B,C,D,E, F,J,K	Put a RANDOMIZE statement (e.g., 90 RANDOMIZE) in the program *before* any RND functions are used.
L	Use RND(1).

A-21 PRODUCE THE SAME SEQUENCE OF RANDOM NUMBERS

Computer	Instructions
A	Use RND(1) on first call of random numbers and RND(0) thereafter.
B,C,F,K,L	Use RND(0).
D,E,J	Use RND.
G,H,I	Use RND(−1) on first call of random numbers and RND(0) thereafter.

A-22 BLANK FORM FOR COMPUTERS NOT LISTED IN A-1

Sign-on instructions

Sign-off instructions

Display the program in work space

Execute the program in work space

Clear out the program in work space

Jump out of an input loop

Interrupt a running program

Delete a character while typing

Delete an entire line while typing

Respond to system error messages

Move a program from memory to work space

Move a program from work space to memory

Clear out a program in memory

Name a program in work space

Display a catalog of programs in account

Mth through Nth characters of string A$

Convert position number to corresponding character in ASCII set

Convert character to equivalent position number in ASCII set

Produce a different sequence of random numbers

_____

_____

Produce the same sequence of random numbers

_____

_____

APPENDIX B
Glossary

ABS(X)

A BASIC function that takes the absolute value of X. Positive values of X remain positive. Negative values of X become positive.

Arithmetic Operators

Addition +, subtraction −, multiplication *, division /, and exponentiation ↑.

asc(A$)

A BASIC function that converts the first character in A$ to its equivalent position number in the ASCII character set. The function may have different forms on different computers. See Appendix A for details.

BASIC

An acronynm for "Beginners All-Purpose Instruction Code". More people know how to program computers in BASIC than any other lanquage.

chr$(N)

A BASIC function that returns the Nth character from the ASCII character set. The function may have different forms on different computers. See Appendix A for details.

Control Characters

These are characters typed on a computer terminal while holding the CONTROL or CTRL key down. They are used to send special signals to the computer.

DATA

A statement used to hold information within a program. This information is called for with a READ statement.

DEF

A BASIC statement used to define functions which are lengthy and will be used often in a program.

Deleting BASIC Statements

Type the line number of the statement to be deleted followed by a carriage return.

DIM

A BASIC statement used to specify the size and reserve space for both numeric and string arrays.

Double Subscripts

Indicated within parentheses following a variable name, and separated by a comma. Used to specify a row and column number in an array. A(3,5), for example means the element in the two dimensional array A at row 3 and column 5.

END

Marks the end of a BASIC program. It must have the highest line number in the program. The END statement is optional on most computers.

E Notation

A notation used in BASIC to express either very large or small numbers.

FOR NEXT

Statements used in BASIC to set up loops.

GOSUB

A BASIC statement used to transfer program control to a subroutine.

GOTO

An unconditional branch statement.

INPUT

A statement that calls for input of information from the terminal.

Inserting BASIC Statements

Type in the statement using a line number not already in use.

IF THEN

A conditional branch statement.

INT(X)

A BASIC function that takes the integer part of X. The integer part of X is defined as the first integer than is less that or equal to X.

LEN(A$)

A BASIC function used to determine the length of a string in characters. For example, if A$ = "HOUSE" then LEN(A$) is 5.

LET

Identifies a BASIC assignment statement. It is always followed by a variable name, an equal sign, and a BASIC expression. On most computers the use of the characters LET in the assignment statement is optional.

LIST

A system command used to tell the computer to print out the program in work space.

MAT =

A matrix command used to set one array equal to another term by term. Both arrays must have the name number of rows and columns.

MAT INPUT

A matrix command used to call for the input of all the elements in an array. The elements are typed in at the keyboard.

MAT READ

A matrix command used to call for the input of the elements in an array. The elements are stored in DATA statements.

MAT ZER

A matrix command used to fill an array with zeros.

PRINT

A BASIC statement that sends information from the computer to the terminal.

Numeric Variable Names

All computers permit either a single letter or a single letter followed by a single digit. Most of the newer computers permit "long" names.

Random Numbers

A sequence of numbers generated by the RND function. They appear to have no pattern or relationship to one another.

READ

A statement that calls for input of information stored in DATA statements within the program.

Replacing BASIC Statements

Retype the statement to be replaced including the line number.

RETURN

A BASIC statement used to transfer program control back from a subroutine to the main program.

RND

A BASIC function used to generate random numbers.

RUN

A system command used to tell the computer to begin execution of the program in work space.

SGN(X)

A BASIC function that determines the sign of X. SGN(X) is +1, 0, −1 as X is positive, zero, or negative respectively.

Single Subscripts

Indicated within parentheses following a variable name. Used to specify a particular element in an array. A(6), for example, means the sixth element of the one dimensional array A.

SQR(X)

A BASIC function that takes the square root of X. X cannot be negative.

Terminal

A typewriter-like device used to communicate with a computer. It can send messages to, or recieve messages from a computer.

Practice Test Solutions

Chapter 2

1. See Appendix A.

2. See Appendix A.

3. Press the RETURN key.

4. See Appendix A.

5. See Appendix A.

6. The line PRINT C has no line number.

7. No END statement.

8. Type the line number and press the RETURN key.

9. Type the line using a line number not already in the program.

10. Retype the line including the line number.

11. See Appendix A.

12. See Appendix A.

13. See Appendix A.

Chapter 3

1. a. −   b. *   c. +   d. ↑ or ∧   e. /

2. a. Exponentiation b. Multiplication and division c. Addition and subtraction

Practice Test Solutions **285**

3. Left to right.

4.

$$100 \text{ LET } A = (4+3*B/D)^2$$

5. 4

6. a. 5.16E+06   b. 3.14E-05

7. a. 7258000 b. 0.001437

8. / then + then ↑

9. A single letter or a single letter followed by a single digit.

10. See Appendix A.

11. See Appendix A.

Chapter 4

1.
```
   1        2        3        4        5
   6        7        8        9       10
  11       12       13       14       15
  16       17       18       19       20
STOP
```

2. a. By assignment (e.g., 100 LET A = 3) b. INPUT statements c. READ and DATA statements

3. A string.

4. To provide information within the program for the benefit of the programmer or user.

5. DATA.

6. Y = 3 will be printed out.

7. Five.

8. As many as needed.

9. To provide a method to obtain variable spacing in the output.

10.   1   3
         1   3

11.   ?10,12,13
         EXTRA INPUT - WARNING ONLY
         22

12.   100 PRINT "INPUT NO. OF MILES";
         110 INPUT N
         120 LET K = 1.609*N
         130 PRINT N;" MILES EQUALS ";K
         140 PRINT "KILOMETERS"
         150 END

Chapter 5

1.   6
         10
         14
         18

2.   BEST

         BETTER
         BEST

         GOOD
         BETTER
         BEST

         OUT OF DATA IN LINE 100

3.   100 PRINT "HOW MANY WIDGETS";
         110 INPUT N
         120 IF N <= 20 THEN 160
         130 IF N <= 50 THEN 180
         140 LET U = 1.5
         150 GOTO 190
         160 LET U = 2
         170 GOTO 190
         180 LET U = 1.8
         190 LET P = N*U
         200 PRINT "PRICE PER WIDGET IS ";U
         210 PRINT "TOTAL COST OF ORDER IS";P

```
220 PRINT
230 GOTO 100
240 END
```

4.
```
100 LET X = 0
110 PRINT X,
120 LET X = X+5
130 IF X <= 170 THEN 110
140 END
```

5.
```
100 PRINT "WHAT WAS SPEED LIMIT ";
110 INPUT A
120 PRINT "SPEED ARRESTED AT ";
130 INPUT B
140 LET X = B-A
150 IF X <= 10 THEM 210
160 IF X <= 20 THEN 230
170 IF X <= 30 THEN 250
180 IF X <= 40 THEN 270
190 LET F = 80
200 GOTO 280
210 LET F = 5
220 GOTO 280
230 LET F = 10
240 GOTO 280
250 LET F = 20
260 GOTO 280
270 LET F = 40
280 PRINT "FINE IS ";F;" DOLLARS"
290 END
```

Chapter 6

1.   20   18   16   14   12
         10   8   6   4   2

2.   1   2   3   2   4
         6   3   6   9   4
         8   12

3. a. 6 b. 7   c. 22.8   d. −1

4. The loops are crossed.

5.
```
100 PRINT "MILES","KILOMETERS"
110 PRINT
120 FOR M = 10 TO 100 STEP 5
130 PRINT M,1.609*M
140 NEXT M
150 END
```

6.
```
100 DATA 10
110 DATA 25,21,24,21,26,27,25,24,23,24
120 READ N
130 LET S = 0
140 FOR I = 1 TO N
150 READ X
160 LET S = S+X
170 NEXT I
180 PRINT S/N
190 END
```

Chapter 7

1. To save space for an array.

2. X(3,4)

3.
```
100 DIM A(8)
110 MAT READ A
```

4.
```
100 DIM A(50)
110 PRINT "HOW MANY NUMBERS ";
120 INPUT N
130 PRINT "WHAT ARE THE NUMBERS";
140 MAT INPUT A(N)
150 LET S = 0
160 FOR I = 1 TO N
170 IF A(I) <= 0 THEN 190
180 LET S = S+A(I)
190 NEXT I
200 PRINT "SUM OF POSITIVE ELEMENTS IS ";S
210 END
```

5. To assign all the elements in an array equal to 0.

6.
```
100 FOR R = 1 TO 4
110 FOR C = 1 TO 6
120 LET X(R,C) = 4
130 NEXT C
140 NEXT R
150 END
```

Practice Test Solutions

7.
2	0	0	0	0
0	2	0	0	0
0	0	2	0	0
0	0	0	2	0
0	0	0	0	2

8. a. 100 DIM A(2,3) b. A(2,3) = 4 c. A(X,Y) = A(1,2) = 3 d. A(A(1,1), A(2,2)) = A(1,2) = 3

Chapter 8

1. By appending $ to a numeric variable name.

2. To set an upper limit on the length in characters of a string.

3. False

4. seg(A$,5,13)

5.
```
100 DIM A$(72)
110 INPUT A$
120 FOR X = LEN(A$) TO 1 STEP -1
130 PRINT seg(A$,1,X)
140 NEXT X
150 END
```

6.
```
a
ab
abc
abcd
abcde
        etc.
abcdefghijklmnopqrstuvwxyz
```

Chapter 9

1. a. 4 b. 14 c. 30 d. 80

2.   2   1   3
       4

3. a. Type in GOSUB (line number at beginning of subroutine) b. RETURN c. To prevent the computer from falling into the subroutine

290   BASIC: A Hands-on Method

4.   WHITE
           RED
           BLUE

Chapter 10

1.   100 FOR I = 1 TO 100
           110 LET X = INT(4*RND(0)+1)
           120 PRINT X,
           130 NEXT I
           140 END

2.   100 FOR I = 1 TO 100
           110 LET X = 25+25*RND(0)
           120 PRINT X,
           130 NEXT I
           140 END

3. The output will be randomly selected from WHITE and RED. Three program outputs are shown to indicate the random nature of the process.

```
           (1)                 (2)                 (3)
           RED                 WHITE               WHITE
           RED                 WHITE               RED
           WHITE               RED                 WHITE
           WHITE               WHITE               WHITE
           RED                 WHITE               WHITE
           RED                 RED                 WHITE
           RED                 RED                 RED
           WHITE               RED                 WHITE
           RED                 WHITE               WHITE
           RED                 WHITE               RED
```

4. Five random numbers of the form X.XX over the range 0.00 to 9.99. Three program outputs are shown below to illustrate the random nature of the process.

```
           (1)                 (2)                 (3)
           .51                 6.69                1.15
           9.34                4.04                8.87
           9.08                9.06                9.26
           9.26                6.71                2.59
           5.98                8.15                3.05
```

Solutions To Odd-Numbered Problems

Chapter 4

1.
```
100 REM CHAP 4, PROB 1
110 READ A,B,C,D
120 DATA 10,9,1,2
130 LET S = A+B
140 LET P = C*D
150 PRINT S,P
160 END
```

3.
```
100 REM CHAP 4, PROB 3
110 READ A,B,C,D
120 DATA 21,18,6,3
130 PRINT A
140 PRINT B
150 PRINT C
160 PRINT D
170 END
```

5. There is no value assigned to C.

7.
```
100 REM CHAP 4, PROB 7
110 PRINT "CASH = ";
120 INPUT C
130 PRINT "MARKETABLE SECURITIES = ";
140 INPUT M
150 PRINT "RECEIVABLES =";
160 INPUT R
170 PRINT "LIABILITIES = ";
180 INPUT L
190 LET A = (C+M+R)/L
200 PRINT "ACID-TEST RATIO = ";A
210 END
```

9. The program loops back to line 100 where A is set equal to 1 after each printout. The program can be corrected by changing line 130 to READ.

```
130 GOTO 110
```

11. The problem lies in statements 100, 110, and 120. The values of L, W, and H are supposed to be printed out, but they haven't been defined. One of two things will happen; either the computer will signal an error and stop or will assign the value zero to the three variables and proceed to line 130. Either way it isn't what is desired. The program will work if the variables are deleted from the ends of the PRINT statements in lines 100, 110, and 120.

13.
```
100 REM CHAP 4, PROB 13
110 DATA 21423,21493,5
120 DATA 5270,5504,13
130 DATA 65214,65559,11.5
140 READ R1,R2,G
150 LET M = (R2-R1)/G
160 PRINT M
170 GOTO 140
180 END
```

15.
```
100 REM CHAP 4, PROB 15
110 DATA 92,63,75,82,72,53,100,89,70,81
120 READ A,B,C,D,E,F,G,H,I,J
130 PRINT (A+B+C+D+E+F+G+H+I+J)/10
140 END
```

17.
```
100 REM CHAP 4, PROB 17
110 PRINT "QUOTED INTEREST RATE (PERCENT) "
120 INPUT R
130 PRINT "NUMBER OF TIMES COMPOUNDED PER YEAR "
140 INPUT M
150 LET T = ((1+R/(100*M))^M-1)*100
160 PRINT "TRUE ANNUAL INTEREST RATE IS "
170 PRINT T
180 END
```

19.
```
100 REM CHAP 4, PROB 19
110 PRINT "INITIAL INBESTMENT ";
120 INPUT P
130 PRINT "ANNUAL INTEREST RATE(%) ";
140 INPUT I
150 PRINT "YEARS LEFT TO ACCRUE INTEREST ";
```

```
160 INPUT N
170 LET T = P*(1+I/100)^N
180 PRINT "TOTAL VALUE IS ";T
190 END
```

Chapter 5

1.
```
100 REM CHAP 5, PROB 1
110 INPUT X,Y
120 IF X>Y THEN 150
130 PRINT Y
140 GOTO 160
150 PRINT X
160 END
```

3.
```
100 REM CHAP 5, PROB 3
110 LET S = 0
120 LET X = 1
130 LET S = S+X
140 LET X = X+1
150 IF X <= 100 THEN 130
160 PRINT S
170 END
```

5.   OUT OF DATA IN LINE 120

7.
```
100 REM CHAP 5, PROB 7
110 LET S = 0
120 READ X
130 IF X = 9999 THEN 180
140 IF X<-10 THEN 120
150 IF X>10 THEN 120
160 LET S = S+X
170 GOTO 120
180 PRINT S
190 DATA -1,22,17,-6,4,7,9999
200 END
```

9.
```
100 REM CHAP 5, PROB 9
110 LET C = 1
120 LET T = 0
130 LET W = 1
140 LET T = T+W
150 LET C = C+1
160 LET W = 2*W
```

```
          170 IF C <= 22 THEN 140
          180 PRINT T/100
          190 END
```

11. The number 83 will be printed out. The program finds the largest number contained in the two DATA statements.

13.
```
          100 REM CHAP 5, PROB 13
          110 PRINT "LIST PRICE ($) ";
          120 INPUT L
          130 PRINT "DISCOUNT RATE (%) ";
          140 INPUT R
          150 LET D = L*(1 - R/100)
          160 PRINT "DISCOUNTED PRICE IS"
          170 PRINT D;" DOLLARS"
          180 END
```

15.
```
          100 REM CHAP 5, PROB 15
          110 INPUT A,B
          120 IF A >= 10 THEN 130
          121 GOTO 150
          130 IF B >= 10 THEN 140
          131 GOTO 150
          140 PRINT A+B
          141 GOTO 210
          150 IF A < 10 THEN 160
          151 GOTO 180
          160 IF B < 10 THEN 170
          161 GOTO 180
          170 PRINT A*B
          171 GOTO 210
          180 IF A < B THEN 200
          190 PRINT A-B
          191 GOTO 210
          200 PRINT B-A
          210 END
```

17.
```
     100 REM CHAP 5, PROB 17
     110 PRINT "GROWTH RATE (%) ";
     120 INPUT R
     130 LET N = 0
     140 LET Q = 1
     150 LET Q = Q*(1+R/100)
     160 LET N = N+1
     170 IF Q <= 2 THEN 150
     180 PRINT "NUMBER OF GROWTH PERIODS TO DOUBLE IS ";N
     190 END
```

19.
```
100 REM CHAP 5, PROB 19
110 PRINT "N = ";
120 INPUT N
130 LET T = 1
140 LET S = 0
150 LET S = S+1/T
160 LET T = T+1
170 IF T <= N THEN 150
180 PRINT "SUM OF ";N;" TERMS IS ";S
190 END
```

Chapter 6

1.
```
100 REM CHAP 6, PROB 1
110 PRINT "N","SQR(N)"
120 PRINT
130 FOR N = 2 TO 4 STEP .1
140 PRINT N,SQR(N)
150 NEXT N
160 END
```

3.
```
100 REM CHAP 6, PROB 3
110 INPUT N
120 LET X = 2 TO N STEP 2
130 PRINT X
140 NEXT X
150 END
```

5.
```
          ABCDEFGHIJ
         ABCDEFGHIJ
        ABCDEFGHIJ
       ABCDEFGHIJ
      ABCDEFGHIJ
     ABCDEFGHIJ
    ABCDEFGHIJ
   ABCDEFGHIJ
  ABCDEFGHIJ
 ABCDEFGHIJ
```

7. Nothing will be printed out! The Z and V loops are crossed.

9. It reads and prints out five numbers rounded off to two places past the decimal point.

11.   6,12
       3
       4
       5
       0

13.   100 REM CHAP 6, PROB 13
       110 INPUT N
       120 INPUT X
       130 LET L = X
       140 LET H = X
       150 LET S = X
       160 FOR I = 1 TO N-1
       170 INPUT X
       180 IF X > L THEN 200
       190 LET L = X
       200 IF X < H THEN 220
       210 LET H = X
       220 LET S = S+X
       230 NEXT I
       240 PRINT "HIGHEST GRADE IS ";H
       250 PRINT "LOWEST GRADE IS ";L
       260 PRINT "AVERAGE IS ";S/N
       270 END

15.   1   2   3
       2   4   6
       3   6   9
       4   8   12

17.   100 REM CHAP 6, PROB 17
       110 READ N
       120 FOR I = 1 TO N
       130 READ M,R,D1,D2,D3,D4,D5
       140 PRINT "EMPLOYEE NUMBER ";M
       150 LET H = D1+D2+D3+D4+D5
       160 IF H <= 40 THEN 180
       170 LET P = R*40 + 1.5*R*(H-40)
       175 GOTO 185
       180 LET P = R*H
       185 PRINT "PAY IS ";P
       187 NEXT I
       190 DATA 5
       200 DATA 2,4.8,8,10,8,7,10
       201 DATA 5,3.75,7,8,8,6,10
       202 DATA 1,3.25,8,10,6,8,8
       203 DATA 4,5,8,10,6,10,6
       204 DATA 3,4.25,6,6,8,10,7
       210 END

Chapter 7

1.
```
100 REM CHAP 7, PROB 1
110 DIM X(20)
120 READ N
130 FOR I = 1 TO N
150 READ X(I)
160 NEXT I
170 FOR I = 1 TO N
180 PRINT X(I)
190 NEXT I
200 DATA 12
210 DATA 2,1,4,3,2,4,5,6,3,5,4,1
220 END
```

3.
```
100 REM CHAP 7, PROB 3
110 DIM A(10,10)
120 INPUT N
130 FOR R = 1 TO N
140 FOR C = 1 TO N
150 INPUT A(R,C)
160 NEXT C
170 NEXT R
180 LET S = 0
190 FOR I = 1 TO N
200 LET S = S + A(I,I)
210 NEXT I
220 PRINT "SUM OF MAIN DIAGONAL IS ";S
230 END
```

5.
```
100 REM CHAP 7, PROB 5
110 DIM A(15,15)
120 INPUT M,N
130 FOR R = 1 TO M
140 FOR C = 1 TO N
150 INPUT A(R,C)
160 NEXT C
170 NEXT R
180 LET S = 0
190 FOR R = 1 TO M
200 FOR C = 1 TO N
210 LET S = S+A(R,C)
220 NEXT C
230 NEXT R
240 PRINT "SUM OF ENTRIES IS ";S
250 END
```

7.   10

9.   16

11.
```
100 REM CHAP 7, PROB 11
110 DIM X(100)
120 INPUT N
130 MAT INPUT X(N)
140 FOR I = 1 TO N-1
150 IF X(I+1) <= X(I) THEN 200
160 LET T = X(I+1)
170 LET X(I+1) = X(I)
180 LET X(I) = T
190 GOTO 140
200 NEXT I
210 MAT PRINT X
220 END
```

13.

1	1	1	1	1	1
0	0	0	0	0	0
0	0	1	1	1	1
0	0	0	0	0	0
0	0	0	0	1	1
0	0	0	0	0	0

15.
```
100 REM CHAP 7, PROB 15
110 DIM X(2,5)
120 MAT READ X
130 DATA 2,1,0,5,1
140 DATA 3,2,1,3,1
150 MAT PRINT X;
160 END
```

17.
```
100 REM CHAP 7, PROB 17
110 DIM X(20,20)
120 INPUT M,N
130 MAT INPUT X(M,N)
140 FOR R = 1 TO M
```

```
150 LET S = 0
160 FOR C = 1 TO N
170 LET S = S+X(R,C)
180 NEXT C
190 PRINT "SUM OF ROW ";R;" IS ";S
200 NEXT R
210 FOR C = 1 TO N
220 LET P = 1
230 FOR R = 1 TO M
240 LET P = P*X(R,C)
250 NEXT R
260 PRINT "PRODUCT OF COLUMN ";C;" IS ";P
270 NEXT C
280 END
```

19.
```
100 REM CHAP 7, PROB 19
110 DIM X(4,6)
120 MAT READ X
130 DATA 48,40,73,120,100,90
140 DATA 75,130,90,140,110,85
150 DATA 50,72,140,125,106,92
160 DATA 108,75,92,152,91,87
170 FOR C = 1 TO 6
180 LET S = 0
190 FOR R = 1 TO 4
200 LET S = S+X(R,C)
210 NEXT R
220 PRINT "TOTAL-DAY ";C;" IS ";S
230 NEXT C
235 PRINT
240 FOR R = 1 TO 4
250 LET S = 0
260 FOR C = 1 TO 6
270 LET S = S+X(R,C)
280 NEXT C
290 PRINT "TOTAL-SALESPERSON ";R;" IS ";S
300 NEXT R
310 LET S = 0
320 FOR R = 1 TO 4
330 FOR C = 1 TO 6
340 LET S = S+X(R,C)
350 NEXT C
360 NEXT R
365 PRINT
370 PRINT "TOTAL SALES FOR THE WEEK IS ";S
380 END
```

21.
```
100 REM CHAP 7, PROB 21
110 DIM P(20),X(20)
120 PRINT "HOW LONG ARE THE ARRAYS ";
130 INPUT N
140 FOR I = 1 TO N
150 LET P(I) = I
160 NEXT I
170 MAT INPUT X(N)
180 FOR I = 1 TO N-1
190 IF X(P(I))>X(P(I+1)) THEN 240
200 LET T = P(I)
210 LET P(I) = P(I+1)
220 LET P(I+1) = T
230 GOTO 180
240 NEXT I
250 PRINT "P","X"
260 PRINT
270 FOR I = 1 TO N
280 PRINT P(I),X(I)
290 NEXT I
300 END
```

Chapter 8.

1.
```
100 REM CHAP 8, PROB 1
110 DIM A$(72)
120 INPUT A$
130 FOR I = 1 TO LEN(A$)
140 PRINT seg(A$,I,I)
150 NEXT I
160 END
```

3.
```
100 REM CHAP 8, PROB 3
110 DIM A$(72)
120 INPUT A$
130 LET A = 0
140 LET E = 0
150 LET I = 0
160 LET O = 0
170 LET U = 0
180 FOR I = I TO LEN(A$)
190 IF seg(A$,I,I) = "A" THEN 250
200 IF seg(A$,I,I) = "E" THEN 270
210 IF seg(A$,I,I) = "I" THEN 290
220 IF seg(A$,I,I) = "O" THEN 310
230 IF seg(A$,I,I) = "U" THEN 330
240 GOTO 340
250 LET A = A+1
260 GOTO 340
```

```
270 LET E = E+1
280 GOTO 340
290 LET I = I+1
300 GOTO 340
310 LET O = O+1
320 GOTO 340
330 LET U = U+1
340 NEXT I
350 PRINT "A = ";A
360 PRINT "E = ";E
370 PRINT "I = ";I
380 PRINT "O = ";O
390 PRINT "U = ";U
400 END
```

5.
```
100 REM CHAP 8 PROB 5
110 DIM A$(72),B$(72)
120 INPUT A$
130 LET J = 1
140 FOR I = 1 TO LEN(A$)
150 IF seg(A$,I,I) = chr$(32) THEN 180
160 LET seg(B$,J,J) = seg(A$,I,I)
170 LET J = J+1
180 NEXT I
190 PRINT B$
200 END
```

7.
```
100 REM CHAP 8, PROB 7
110 DIM A$(72)
120 LET C = 0
130 FOR K = 1 TO 5
140 INPUT A$
150 IF seg(A$,1,4)<>"THE " THEN 170
160 LET C = C+1
170 FOR I = 2 TO LEN(A$)-3
180 IF seg(A$,I,I+3)<>" THE " THEN 200
190 LET C = C+1
200 NEXT I
210 PRINT C
220 END
```

9.
```
100 REM CHAP 8; PROB 9
110 DIM A$(72)
120 INPUT A$
130 LET C = 0
140 FOR K = 1 TO LEN(A$)-1
150 IF seg(A$,K,K+1)<>"IN" THEN 170
```

```
160 LET C = C+1
170 NEXT K
180 PRINT C
190 END
```

Chapter 9

1.   25   5   20
    65

3.
```
100 REM CHAP 9, PROB 3
110 DEF FNA(R) = 3.14159*R^2
120 DEF FNB(R) = 4*3.14159*R^3/3
130 PRINT
140 PRINT "R","AREA OF","VOLUME OF"
150 PRINT " ","CIRCLE","SPHERE"
160 PRINT
170 FOR R = 1 TO 10 STEP .5
180 PRINT R,FNA(R),FNB(R)
190 NEXT R
200 END
```

5.   55
       15
       36

7.
```
500 REM SUBROUTINE
510 LET L = X(2)
520 FOR I = 3 TO X(1)+1
530 IF L >= X(I) THEN 550
540 LET L = X(I)
550 NEXT I
560 RETURN
```

9.
```
900 REM SUBROUTINE
910 LET S1 = 0
920 LET S2 = 0
930 FOR I = 2 TO Y(1)+1
940 LET S1 = S1+Y(I)
950 LET S2 = S2+Y(I)^2
960 NEXT I
970 LET M = S1/Y(1)
```

Solutions to Odd-Numbered Problems **303**

```
980 LET S = SQR((Y(1)*S2-S1^2)/(Y(1)*(Y(1)-1)))
990 RETURN
```

Chapter 10

1.
```
100 REM CHAP 10, PROB 1
110 FOR I = 1 TO 25
120 LET N = INT(100*RND(0))/10
130 PRINT N,
140 NEXT I
150 END
```

3. A typical output is:

.04	.02	.17	.14	.01
.03	.16	.04.	.05	.17
.19	.12	.07	.11	.19
.11	.19	.2	.18	.04

5.
```
100 REM CHAP 10, PROB 5
110 FOR I = 1 TO 5
120 READ N
130 LET H = 0
140 LET T = 0
150 FOR J = 1 TO N
160 LET X = INT(2*RND(0)+1)
170 IF X = 1 THEN 200
180 LET T = T+1
190 GOTO 210
200 LET H = H+1
210 NEXT J
220 PRINT
230 PRINT "FOR ";N;" TOSSES THERE WERE"
240 PRINT H;" HEADS AND ";T;" TAILS"
250 NEXT I
260 DATA 10,50,100,500,1000
270 END
```

7.
```
100 REM CHAP 10, PROB 7
110 LET S = 0
120 FOR I = 1 TO 1000
130 LET S = S+RND(0)
140 NEXT I
150 PRINT S/1000
160 END
```

9.
```
100 REM CHAP 10, PROB 9
110 LET M = 0
120 FOR I = 1 TO 1000
130 LET A = 60*RND(0)
140 LET B = 60*RND(0)
150 IF ABS(A-B)>10 THEN 170
160 LET M = M+1
170 NEXT I
180 PRINT "PROBABILITY OF A MEET IS ";M/1000
190 END
```

11.
```
100 REM CHAP 10, PROB 11
110 FOR I = 1 TO 25
120 LET S = 0
130 FOR J = 1 TO 12
140 LET S = S+RND(0)
150 NEXT J
160 LET R = 10+2*(S-6)
170 PRINT INT(100*R+.5)/100,
180 NEXT I
190 END
```

Index

ABS, 152
Arithmetic in BASIC, 46
Arithmetic, priority, 47
Array Operations, program, 197
Arrays, 170
asc, 220
ASCII character set, 220, 221
Automobile License Fees, program, 110
Averaging Numbers, program, 114

BASIC, arithmetic, 46
BASIC functions,
    ABS, 152
    asc, 220
    chr$, 220
    INT, 150
    LEN, 218
    RND, 261
    SGN, 151
    SQR, 150
    TAB, 80
BASIC, origins, 2
BASIC, parentheses, 49
BASIC programs,
    Array Operations, 197
    Averaging Numbers, 114
    Automobile License Fees, 110
    Birthday Pairs in a Crowd, 266
    Carpet Estimating, 243
    catalog, 55
    Converting Temperature, 85
    Course Grades, 193
    Depreciation Schedule, 158
    Distribution of Random Numbers, 265
    Exact Division, 156
    Examination Grades, 190
    Finding the Average of a Group of Numbers, 153
    Flipping Coins, 263
    Printout of Number Patterns, 109
    Random Integers, 264
    Replacement Code, 222
    requirements, 24
    retrieval, 54
    Rounding Off Dollar Values to Cents, 240
    storage, 54
    String Reversal, 220
    Sum and Product of Numbers, 86
    Temperature Conversion Table, 155
    Unit Prices, 82
    Word Count, 222
BASIC statements,
    DATA, 76
    DEF, 236
    DIM, 184
    END, 24
    FOR NEXT, 145
    GOSUB, 239
    GOTO, 104
    IF THEN, 105
    INPUT, 76
    LET, 76
    line number, 25
    MAT, 186
    order, 25
    READ, 76
    REM, 81
    RETURN, 240
    translation, 117
BASIC variables, names, 51
Birthday Pairs in a Crowd, program, 266

Carpet Estimating, program, 243
Catalog of BASIC programs, 55

Character deletion, 30
chr$, 220
Conditional transfer, 105
Converting Temperature, program, 85
Course Grades, program, 193
Crossed loops, 148
CRT terminal, 4

DATA, 76
DEF, 236
Depreciation Schedule, program, 158
DIM, 184, 217
Discovery method, 1
Distribution of Random Numbers,
 program, 265

END, 24
E Notation, 50
Error correction, 30
Exact Division, program, 156
Examination Grades, program, 190

Finding the Average of a Group of
 Numbers, program, 153
Flipping Coins, program, 263
FOR NEXT, 145

GOSUB, 239
GOTO, 104

Hard-copy terminal, 4

IF THEN, 105
INPUT, 76
INT, 150

LEN, 218
LET, 76
Line deletion, 32
LIST, 25
Loops, crossed, 148
Loops, FOR NEXT, 148

MAT, 186
MAT INPUT, 187
MAT PRINT, 188
MAT READ, 187
Matrix, 170
Matrix commands, 186
MAT ZER, 186

Parentheses, 49
Printout of Number Patterns,
 program, 109
Printout, spacing, 78
Priority of operations, 47

Random Integers, program, 264
Random numbers, 254
READ, 76
REM, 81
Replacement Code, program, 222
RETURN, 240
RETURN, key, 25
Retrieval of BASIC programs, 54
RND, 261
Rounding Off Dollar Values to
 Cents, program, 240
RUN, 26

Signing on, 10
SGN, 151
Spacing of printout, 78
SQR, 150
Standard deviation, 262
Storage of BASIC programs, 54
String, output, 78
String Reversal, program, 220
String variables, definition, 217
String variables, DIM, 217
Subscripts, 170, 182
Subroutines, 238
Substrings, 219
Sum and Product of Numbers,
 program, 86
System commands,
 LIST, 25
 RUN, 26

TAB, 80
Teletype terminal, 4
Temperature Conversion Table,
 program, 155
Terminal,
 CRT, 4
 hard-copy, 4
 teletype, 4
Tracing programs, 118
Transfer,
 conditional, 105
 unconditional, 104
Translating BASIC statements, 117
Troubleshooting programs, 117

Unconditional transfer, 104
Unit Prices, program, 82

Variable names, 51
Variables, subscripted, 182

Word Count, program, 222
Work space, 25